MW00441742

PRAISE FOR *YOU DO YOU(ISH)*

"It's about frickin' time! *You Do You(ish)* is the book we've desperately needed for so long. Erin brings the fun and sass you'd expect from your best friend, along with the credibility and results of a CEO badass. If you've ever felt like you needed a playbook to cut through the BS in Corporate America, to have a big career without compromising your soul, this book is a must read!"

-Shelley Paxton, Former CMO Harley Davidson
& Author of *Soulbbatical*

"I've always believed that authenticity has contributed to my career success. Erin gives people more than just permission to be themselves though. *You Do You(ish)* lays out a clear business case for authenticity and gives you an actual playbook to purposefully use authenticity to fuel success. Genius! See how shedding the burden of a persona that isn't you can elicit refreshing achievement."

- Jean LaTorre, EVP and CIO of Guardian

"If you've ever felt like your career and your life are one big teeter-totter ... that you have to trade one for the other ... this is the book for you! Erin brings her notoriously authentic style to *You Do You(ish)* and puts a formula to career success that is refreshing and that anyone can follow."

- Tameeka Smith, CEO, Virginia Community
& State United Healthcare

"WOW! There are so few times that you get honest and impactful career suggestions that are direct and delivered in a fun and caring way. Most of us just stay on the corporate machine but the greatest achievements come from those that leverage the strategies that Erin so genuinely shares."

~ Steve Auerbach, CEO of Alegeus

"*You Do You(ish)* is hilarious, clever, and insightful. Erin delivers authentic, unfiltered, tough-love career coaching that puts a formula to how to have success, without compromising everything else. It's a must-read for anyone; from people just starting out in their career to seasoned executives. She is simply real. It's so refreshing to have a business book that's both impactful and fun to read!"

~ Renee Zaugg, CIO, Otis Elevator

YOU DO YOU(ish)

YOU DO YOU(ish)

UNLEASH YOUR AUTHENTIC SUPERPOWERS TO GET THE CAREER YOU DESERVE

ERIN HATZIKOSTAS

b Authentic Inc Publishing

b Authentic Inc Publishing

Contact info: hello@bauthenticinc.com

978-1-7363765-0-8 (paperback)

978-1-7363765-1-5 (eBook)

Library of Congress Control Number: 2021901478

Book design: Dino Marino

Cover design: Rejenne Pavon

BIO

Former Corporate CEO turned Professional Pot-Stirrer, Erin Hatzikostas, is on a hell-bent mission to help people have the big career they deserve, without compromising everything else. She's the friend, mom, coach, guru, and boss you always wanted, all rolled into one. Erin became a CEO at 42 – yet she smashes open the executive mold. She is most regarded for her Midwestern-inspired, unpretentious, witty, and authentic style of leadership. She is an author, career coach, TEDx speaker, podcast co-host, mom, wife, runner, skier, and someone who loves doing the Running Man dance anywhere she's not supposed to.

DEDICATION

To my father, whose authenticity laid the foundation for my obsession. And to my mother for putting up with this authenticity for fifty years and counting. I love you both.

To my mini-humans, Ella and Mick.
You inspire me more than you know.

And to my husband, Manny.
Thank you for loving me. All of me(ish).

Table of Contents

PREFACE(ISH) i

PART 1 – WHO SAYS THOSE ARE THE RULES? 1

1: Don't hate, re-create 2

2: Yep, that wall is real 8

3: Not your mother's career advice 13

4: You don't know whatcha got till it's gone 16

5: This ain't Ikea, people 18

6: Authenticity is ishy 26

7: Data for the doubters 32

8: My ground zero 38

9: The power of a yawn 44

PART 2 – WHO SAYS THAT'S YOUR PLAYLIST? 50

10: Stop, primer time 51

11: Let's get metaphysical, metaphysical. I wanna get metaphysical ... 54

12: Sucky Song #1: I have to compromise my family for my career 58

13: Sucky Song #2: I'm not qualified for the job 65

14: Sucky Song #3: Others have more money, that's why they can do it 74

15: Sucky Song #4: I'm already working too hard, the next level will have me working even harder 83

16: Sucky Song #5: I'm not good at office politics, so I can't play with the big boys and girls 90

PART 3 – WHO SAYS AUTHENTICITY CAN'T BE YOUR SECRET WEAPON? 97

17: We are human after all 98

18: **H**umility: Cooking up some humble pie 101

19: **U**nexpected: The left side love punch they didn't see coming 116

20: **M**odel: Show don't tell 126

21: **A**dapt: Plug and evolve 137

22: **N**arrate: Wake them up before they go-go 147

23: **S**park: Let's light shit on fire! 166

24: Uh, Cliff's Notes please 176

PART 4 – WHO SAYS THIS IS THE TOP? 181

25: Proudest coaching moment ever 182

26: I'm not a unicorn. You don't have to be one either. 185

27: There's no time like the present 194

28: We need a whole bunch of A-HOLEs 196

29: Be your own prince(ss) 199

THE REAL(ISH) PREFACE 205

DISCUSSION GUIDE 208

RESOURCES 210

ABOUT THE AUTHOR 212

ACKNOWLEDGMENTS 214

Preface(ish)

In the days before I worked on this (not quite) preface, I wrote an email to my book coach with this subject line: *I've hit a massive wall.* I told her I felt like I was trying to climb over one of those obstacles in a muddy endurance event and I couldn't plant my first step. She held me up with her words, as she always does, and we agreed to work through it together. That was on Sunday.

Tuesday, we met on Zoom, and I told her, "I know I can do hard things, but …" — I felt disloyal admitting it — "I've fallen out of love with my book."

Then, as good coaches and coachees do, we settled in to talk through my challenges. First, we tackled the issues that were laid bare, those I was keenly aware of because they were glaring at me as I wrote – I was struggling to reorder sections, and my voice wasn't reaching deeply enough into the readers' hearts and minds in some places. Then she nudged me into the place where the mud was plastered on the wall I was trying to climb.

"What's really eating at you, Erin?" she finally asked.

I looked out my office window, got silent for an awkward amount of time, and finally replied, "I loved the book … until … I had to start shaping it into how a *normal* book should be."

The light shines on what you need to see when you allow yourself to go several layers deeper.

I realized that when I got to the part in the process when I was *supposed* to do stuff — when I was *supposed* to write a preface that told you all this crap about what I learned while writing ... when I was *supposed* to create chapters that mirrored how books were typically organized ... when I was *supposed* to make it sound like best-selling books always do.

And there is something I knew about myself that I'd thought might not apply to book writing: When I'm *supposed* to do something, I lose my shit.

With this realized, the remedy was easy. Without a second thought, my coach gave me permission to shake things up. Move the "real" preface to the end. Be okay with the book reading differently than others. Double down on my idea to tell you little stories throughout. And most importantly, to give you the same permission. I lit up. "Really? Well, yeah, I would love to do that!"

So, here's the deal: I finally gave myself the same permission I want to give to you. My entire goal is to help you unlock *authenticity* as your new secret weapon for success in your career. For that reason, I decided it was okay — it was actually necessary — to create an authentic book. To do it my own way.

This book isn't normal. I created it my own way, and I want you to read it your own way. If you're looking for a full-fledged voyage that convinces you of the power of authenticity, primes you for change by ridding you of the Sucky Songs you sing, and offers you a framework for how you can use authenticity to transform your career, I'd love nothing more than for you to read the whole damn thing.

If you're one of those people that skips straight to the end of an email to figure out what the call to action is, then what the heck, go ahead and jump right to Part 3, where I teach you, methodically and simply, how to use authenticity as your new career playbook. (If you do this, you'll be an IGW, but you'll have to read Part 1 to know what that that is.)

If you're the type that just wants to ride the waves of my personal journey to discover the power I believe authenticity has, then simply surf from page to page at whatever pace you like.

Oh, and if you're the traditional type (I suspect you're not though), you're more than welcome to flip all the way back, straight-away, to read the more traditional preface at the end.

I realized that this wall I'd hit with my book was the same-shit-different-day of nearly every other wall I'd hit in my life. When things feel hard to me, it's almost always because I'm trying to do something someone else's way (but don't always realize it). Maybe one day I'll stop plowing into these walls and realize, in real time, that authenticity is always at my disposal. It is almost always my best strategy to climb over walls. Until then, like you, I continue with the learning. And much like my book coach did for me, I hope to hold you up with my words. It's time to get *you* over your own wall.

Get out before you're too crusty

2:00 pm – It was time.

My successor was waiting outside my office. It was time to do the proverbial walk-around and introduce him to everyone in the office.

I got up from my chair and headed out to meet him.

He was clearly excited. Of course he was. This was his first moment as the new CEO of our company.

We made small talk as we walked together through the corn maze of cubicles and offices. I told him how awesome every person was and what they were working on. I was following the corporate playbook, conscious that I was being repetitive, but this was what we were supposed to do. We walked around for about forty minutes. Just as we were nearing the end, I looked down and saw a huge white blob hanging from my hair.

"Oh shit," I said, "that must be dried yogurt. From breakfast. Five hours ago."

Be sure to move on before you (or your hair) get too crusty.

PART 1

Who Says Those Are The Rules?

1

Don't hate, re-create

"Imperfection is beauty, madness is genius, and it's better to be absolutely ridiculous than absolutely boring."

- Marilyn Monroe - actress, model, singer and more quotable than you'd ever imagine

I hate books.

I fully understand that by admitting this to you right here and now I may have lost all credibility about ten hot seconds into this book.

But please, just stick with me for a moment.

It's not that I hate *all* books. I just get really anxious as a reader when I think of the commitment a book requires. *You're telling me that you're teaching me one big thing, but I have to read 273 booooring pages to "get it"?*

I admit it. I'm impatient. Like, mega-impatient. I consider myself an Instant Gratification Whore (IGW). I only drink wine with screw tops. I check my weather app while the meteorologist is talking on TV. My favorite thing to buy is pillows because you get to drive home right away, slap them on a couch or bed, and voila, you have change. You've got something better than it was a few minutes before. And I HATE wallowing in problems. I want to solve them. Immediately.

And most books don't offer the kind of pleasure an IGW demands.

I've attempted to read one too many books that spent way too much time on the problem, leaving me like, "Yeah, no shit there's a problem. How do I actually fix it?!"

I felt that way when I read Sheryl Sandberg's book, *Lean In*. I have tremendous respect for Sheryl and everything she's accomplished. When I picked up her book, I was thinking: *Hell to the yes. Let's talk about the fact that us women are part of the problem and how we can be the solution.* And so I dug in with gusto, poised to change my plan. Change my career. Change me. Change to be whatever she told me was having an impact out there as she saw it.

Unfortunately, what I found instead was a well-laid-out business case that proved, without a shadow of a doubt, that women are fucked in the world of business. And as I kept reading, chapter after chapter, I felt like the little kid in the ice cream store screaming her head off because she's been denied the cone. *What are the solutions, Sheryl? Gimme some calls to action here, please!*

One night a few years ago, I glanced at my nightstand as I was getting ready for bed. A book called *Lead Like a Woman* had been camped out there for a solid three months. Without one page turned. Instead, on it sat two bottles of nail polish and a nail file. I thought, *Yep, that's the truth about how great women lead. By having beautiful nails.*

This is my snarky way of saying that if I'm going to give

twenty plus hours to a book, it better not just try to impress me with words I never use, or talk for hundreds of pages about the problem (and not the solution).

When I left my corporate CEO job to become an entrepreneur and bring more authenticity to the workplace, many people said to me, "You should write a book."

At first I thought, *Hell yeah, I should!*

Then I quickly remembered: I hate books. And if there's one thing I hate more than books, it's a hypocrite.

And yet here I am. Writing an effing book.

But I'm not a hypocrite. I'm just someone who, every day, is learning and relearning what I preach to others.

• • • • • • •

You shouldn't *not* do something because you hate the way it was done before. **Instead, do it your own way.**

• • • • • • • •

One of the game changers for me was *You Are a Badass* by Jen Sincero. It was one of the first nonfiction books I ever read front to back. And then read again. And yet again.

Why? Because it was funny. Its message was powerful. She was self-deprecating. The writing was so frickin' authentic.

It wasn't all, step one, step two, step three.

It wasn't written as if she had a stick up her ass. She didn't pretend to have all the answers. And she certainly didn't leave me wallowing in the problems.

It was lesson number 1,683 in a series of lifetime lessons for me — that a person can rewrite the rules. Duh. *I can write a book my own way.*

And what better way to do it differently than a book about doing your career your own way?

We should spend less time shadowing the old rules and more time shaping the new ones.

Here's the deal I want to make with you …

If you promise to leave the old rules behind …

If you agree to get on board with being a leader, not a follower …

If you commit to shaping the next few decades of workplace rules, alongside me and the others reading this book …

Then I promise to make *You Do You(ish)* only as long as it needs to be.

I promise to spend a hell of a lot more time on the solutions than the problems.

And I most definitely promise not to be snoozy, stuffy, or boring.

Deal?

Deal.

(And if nothing else, you've got another book for your bedside nail polish collection.)

2 Yep, that wall is real

"There's nothing as unstoppable as a freight train full of fuck-yeah."

~ Jen Sincero - my author idol

To steal from Jen Sincero — "You are a badass."

You've worked hard your entire life. You got good grades. You've blown past other people's expectations … probably even your own. You grew up believing in the notion that hard work pays off. And that's not necessarily wrong. And yeah, sure you've heard the "Work smarter, not harder" cliché a thousand times. But honestly, there didn't seem to be a real reward for that.

The rewards always came when you aced a test. When you ran an extra mile. When you took the AP class. Then the rewards kept coming in your work life. When you crushed an assignment. When you worked nights and weekends. When you did anything it took to be the superhero employee of the year. One day you woke up though and realized that chasing these rewards left you feeling like you were running on a treadmill and someone kept hitting the Up button without you knowing it. Again and again and again.

Meanwhile, even though you've moved from healthy jog to nonstop sprint on this treadmill (getting a paycheck every two weeks for incentive), a wall appeared almost out of nowhere. More like, you finally saw the wall that had been in the near distance all along.

Sadly, that wall is real.

That wall has a name: BS Burnout.

Every day you feel like you have to make a choice: Keep running, dismissing the bumps and bruises as you do everything you can to avoid that wall, or hit the wall, fall down, and give up altogether. What's this wall made of? Well, typically it's constructed of things like pressure and politics and PowerPoints … which leave you feeling perplexed, panicked, or even paralyzed (and depending on when you read this, a pandemic is the "icing" on that wall).

You find yourself thinking, *Holy shit, can I do this forever? When am I going to hit my breaking point? Don't I deserve more?*

I'm here to tell you firmly, emphatically, and with all my heart: You do.

But here's what happens to most people. Here's what might happen to you if you don't continue to read this book and believe me when I say that there is a way over this wall. Here's what I dread more than anything in the world: You'll think, *I guess I just need to be okay with "good enough."*

You may have said this already. You might have convinced yourself that despite all the hopes and dreams you laid out after hearing that inspirational graduation speech, you're now okay with having a career that gives you *just* enough … pay, promotion, power. You've decided that you're okay with taking less because taking on more would mean more walls, wouldn't it? Taking on more would mean you'd have to compromise everything else in your life to get more from your career. You've succumbed to the assumption that you'll have to compromise time with your children, with your significant other, and time to stay active and healthy. And most of all, fighting to get over that wall so you can go for the big-girl or big-boy jobs would mean having to compromise something even bigger: your soul.

You're running a common calculation in your head, and you probably didn't even realize it. It's called the Compromise Calculation.

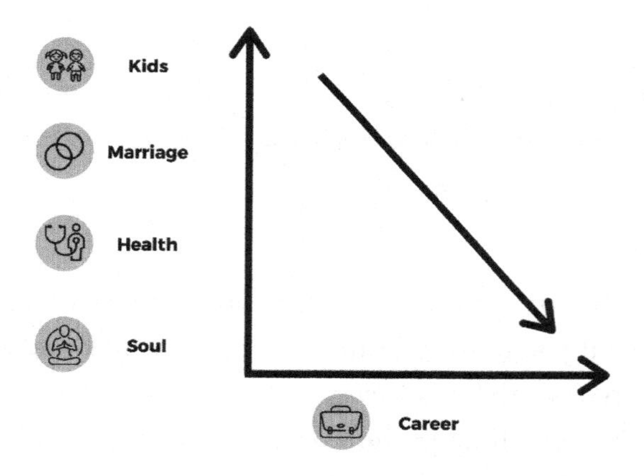

On the x-axis, you have your career. On the y-axis you have everything else in your life (family, friends, health, soul, etc.). In your head, this Compromise Calculation is a hard-coded 45-degree line pointing downward at all times. When your career goes up, everything else goes down. This calculator has you believing that there is a negative correlation between your career success and everything else in life. If this formula was accurate, I wouldn't blame you for a hot second for pulling back on your career (or at minimum, feeling really frickin' frustrated!).

But I'm here to tell you that the Compromise Calculation line is not hard-coded. It can be changed and flipped entirely in the other direction. You can have a *better* overall life while simultaneously crushing your career.

Let me be clear: You can't tip the graph doing the same ole crap you've been doing up until now.

There's good news though: That's exactly what we're going to do together in *You Do You(ish).* I'm going to help you bust down the rugged, sharp, dirty walls that you're running into and that have become the ultimate barrier on your path for success. I'm going to help you rewire your brain and give you permission to do things differently. I'm going to give you the framework, tools, and inspiration to do small experiments that will lead to massive changes. And damn it, I'm going to prove to you that a new path can be paved. You'll be able to lean into your career without compromising everything else.

Stop leaning into your career while leaning out of your life. Instead, it's time to lean in a totally different way altogether.

Rewriting the map of what you thought was your successful career road is, unfortunately, not quite as easy as buying pillows and throwing them on your sofa. Developing a new map takes time. It takes exploration. It takes experimentation. Reflection. Energy. It takes cojones to change what you've learned – and what is believed by an entire system around you – and rewrite the rules. But while it takes time, the strategies I teach are not rocket science. They are not righteous. They are not the stuff of martyrdom. They're fun.

When you read most business books, does it feel like you have to strap yourself in for some sort of noble journey? You task yourself with not only reading the book but also with adopting new behaviors for the greater good. Then while you're reading it, do you start telling yourself that if you could just have a little more discipline, just change who you are, that you'd bring amazing results to your team, boss, organization, and company? (That's so noble of you.) It doesn't have to be this way.

I don't believe in changing people. I believe in changing people's addictions. When you can show someone a new way, give them small experiments, have them experience success, they can't help but become addicted to a new way of being. Get ready to get addicted to authenticity.

3

Not your mother's career advice

"It is better to fail in originality
than to succeed in imitation."

~ Herman Melville - *Moby Dick* author, poet, and a cool old dude

When I leapt from the corporate jungle gym, after twenty-two years swinging around like a contestant on an American Ninja Warrior set, even though leading and inspiring people was kinda my jam, I didn't want any part of it if I had to do it the *normal* way. As you might have already gathered, *normal* is my kryptonite. To me, the career and leadership space felt normal: predictable, by the book, as expected. It kinda felt like executive coaches and leadership-consulting companies were a dime a dozen.

And there's nothing I hate more than being a dime.

So, I forged a different path that checked off more aspirational boxes for me. I started a software company to build an app that helped parents manage their kids' chaotic schedules. Except, I didn't actually *build* anything. While working on that venture, I dabbled at blogging about what I'd learned, sharing the strong opinions I'd formed while running a 9-figure company.

Then one day it dawned on me: *I can do career and leadership. I just have to do it my own frickin' way.* (Like I said earlier, I keep learning and relearning this one.)

Just because there were already thousands of career and leadership companies out there, I didn't have to do it the way any of them were doing it. And hmm ... the more time I spent thinking about it, something made less and less sense. *If there are thousands of companies, books, and coaches out there, why in the hell is the corporate workplace still so effed up?!*

C'mon, you know what I mean: The workplace is largely a disaster. If you're not already with me on that, let me throw a few not-so-super-complex stats at you:

- There are more CEOs named Dave than female CEOs.[1]
- Only about one-third of employees are engaged (read as, *give a shit about their job*).[2]

Note: anywhere you see a cute little superscript number, you can find all the deets in the Resources section at the end of the book.

There might be one thing I hate more than being a dime, and that's an exercise in futility. I feel like that's what the corporate-improvement industry is experiencing today. If we're putting all these companies, this talent, and these books toward bettering the workplace, then why the hell is there still so much suckiness?!

In September 2018, I decided I could in fact take on the career and leadership space. I would just do it my own way. I would create a company that pushed aside all the things that didn't work for me, and bring a fresh approach. I could stand up tall and create a platform that screamed, "Stop the fakeness. Get off the hamster wheel. Knock off the bullshit. There's a better way to do all this!"

Although I followed the corporate path for the first half of my career, the things I coach, teach, and inspire here transcend industries. My corporate friend, I will teach you all my tricks. Or if you're a teacher, you'll be able to better connect with students and administrators. If you run your own business, this book will help your business stand out. If you're an entrepreneur, using the principles in this book will make your business a customer-magnet. And for you, the woman who reluctantly left the working world to help your children get through tough times, I promise my strategies will help you re-enter the workforce when you're ready, in a totally different way than you approached the working world before.

In essence, we *all* have to find a better way. You, dear reader, need to find a better way. Otherwise, well, you're probably going to lose your fucking mind.

4

You don't know whatcha got till it's gone

"Isn't it funny how day by day nothing changes but when you look back everything is different."

~ C.S. Lewis - Novelist, scholar, and broadcaster

I'm not going to say my career was easy, but I distinctly recall many times when I felt guilty that I was having success without all the pain. I'd hear how a colleague canceled a vacation because of a work conflict or how a friend spent the entire weekend working on a project. I knew people who worked hard but were passed up for the promotion they felt they deserved. I'm gonna be honest. I often felt guilty.

I would think to myself, *Why do I keep getting lucky? Why am I not slamming into as many obstacles as those around me? Why do I seem to find success more easily than others?* While I have never been a sloth, and I do have some intellectual chops, I was never a business savant. I didn't come from a long family line of business people. (My parents were teachers.) I grew up in a small town with very limited exposure to the business world I later found myself working in. I'm also sensitive. While I can hit issues head-on, I'd be lying if I said I didn't fear conflict. Most importantly though,

I was never willing to "do whatever it takes" to get the next big job. So I'd wonder sometimes what was driving the success I kept having. I didn't have some secret formula, and I don't believe in pure luck. It had to be something else.

It wasn't until I decided to retire from my corporate job that the answer was revealed. In people's emails, cards, and conversations reacting to my retirement, there was a common thread. Time and time again they used one word. It was of course a word I knew, but not one I had ever attached to myself. People used this word to describe me as an employee *and* as a leader. From this one word, I finally found my answer. From this one word, I also found my obsession. A single word that describes not only what made me beloved but also drove my success. A word that was at the center of what had allowed me to have a big career without compromising everything else. The most powerful win-win word in the English dictionary.

Authenticity.

5

This ain't Ikea, people

"Stay true to yourself, never follow someone else's path. Unless you're in the woods and you're lost and you see a path, then by all means you should follow that."

~ Ellen DeGeneres - comedian, TV show host, actress, writer, producer, and dance-where-you're-not supposed-to compadre

A few years ago, my family and I were in Vermont for a weekend getaway. My husband and I had decided to take the kids out of their regularly scheduled sports-a-palooza to spend some quality time in a place that allowed us to slow down and take a breath.

My seven-year-old son, Mick, asked me to go on a bike ride with him. He and my husband had gone for a ride on the hiking trail down the street earlier that day, and Mick was excited to show me the path they took to a beautiful "pond." We rode for a while and when we got to the pond (which was actually a swamp, but close enough), Mick was so proud to show me what he and his dad had discovered earlier. I'll admit, it was a nice-enough place. But after we stood by our bikes and shared in the view, I said, "Let's go check out some more of the trail. Let's go back to that fork in the path and take a right instead of a left." So, we headed back out. As we rode, it was clear that Mick was getting tired. But every time I offered to turn around and head home, he would say, "No, I'm fine, let's just keep going to the top of that next hill." We rode to the first crest, stopped, and took in the view. I asked him if he wanted to go back. "No, let's just go to that point over there," he said. We did this five, maybe six times until we got to one crest where there was a small waterfall running down to the trail.

Mick was so excited. "Mom, this is so beautiful! I can't wait to tell Daddy what we found!"

My son and husband had found a great path just a few hours earlier. And like so many mentors you've had in your career, Mick's desire was to share his knowledge, to show me his path, so I could enjoy the same success he and his dad had enjoyed. He knew they had success on their bike ride and he wanted to show me the way.

This is what happens with our careers. And it's very well intentioned. And it fucks us up.

People do something. It works out well. They teach others to do it.

The problem is that if you follow someone else's path, you end up doing things that aren't quite right for *you*. Maybe the hills they took were easy for them to pedal up, but for you they're frickin' exhausting. You also limit what is possible for yourself. While the swamp seemed like a perfect destination for Mick earlier that day, because we were curious about other paths, we were able to find an even more beautiful waterfall.

Too often you think of your career like one of those maze puzzles children do on cereal boxes while eating their breakfast.

That you have to find that one perfect path that gets you to "the end." The path that gets you to the optimal level of success you expect for yourself. That end is, of course, different for everyone. For some people, it might be a management job. For others, it could be the CEO of a company. For most people I talk to though, it often comes down to this: They want a "seat at the table." They want to be more than a doer, they want to be a decision maker. They want to have a say in the direction of the organization or the company they're in. They want to influence and inspire others.

But getting there can feel complicated. Making career moves and decisions usually feels incredibly complex. You probably say things to yourself like *What if I make the wrong move and hit a dead end? or What if I go the wrong way and it takes me so much longer to get to "the finish line"?*

When you think about your career, it might also feel like your first time at Ikea. When you go in, you feel beholden to their system. You think that if (heaven forbid) you veer left or right, some store cops will come and reprimand you for careening like a rebel from the living-room section to the home office section without going through the kitchen section. Except, there are no store cops at Ikea. Although there is a beautifully laid-out path, you can go any damn way you please. In fact, if you want, you can walk into the store, take a right instead of a left, and land in the holy land — the warehouse! Your career is no different. Just because you take one path doesn't mean that you can't pivot, skip, jump, bob, weave, veer right, or veer left. In fact, I would argue that your best option is to do all those things.

I want you to understand that the signs and traffic symbols that others have told you are the keys to career success — networking, mentors, executive presence, blah blah blah — are lining a road that certainly worked for others. But there is another beautiful, sassy, fun, and curious path you can take to have career success while also not compromising everything else.

You Do You(ish) is going to shake up everything you've been taught about how to obtain that big-ass career you deserve. I realized that using authenticity in the workplace can be anyone's secret weapon to success. And while that may sound elusive and fluffy, I promise it's not.

Authenticity is powerful for many reasons:

- It allows you to create quicker connections with others.
- People become instantly more curious in who you are, leading to incredible followership (in all directions).
- It activates innovation; the more refreshing and unexpected you act, the more people start to think in refreshing and unexpected ways.
- You start to stand out as a leader and get noticed in ways a resumé or hard work can never do.
- It lights up the people around you. Everyone is yearning to be a bit more human.
- It helps you unlock the power that's sitting dormant inside of you and inside of others.

So, how in the heck will this book help you overcome barriers and crush your career?

Here's the plan …

In Part 1, we're going to dive deep into the definition of "authenticity," first by talking about what authenticity is *not.*

There are so many misconceptions, and I want to wipe the slate clean and define it in a way that makes you go, "Ahh ... that's some badass stuff right there." I'm also going to lay out some data to help you see clear as day that authenticity drives bona fide, money-in-your-pocket success.

In Part 2, before I can teach you a whole new way of workplace being, we'll be getting some shit out of the way by taking a look at the Sucky Songs you're singing to yourself. Every person I know sings at least some of these songs. Hell, I sang a whole slew of Sucky Songs while writing this book. But I realized I was singing them and I rewrote them. I couldn't move on without rewriting them. You can't truly kick some ass without rewriting yours, either. We'll go over the five most common Sucky Songs I hear sung by people stuck in their careers. These tunes are likely the ones you're singin' to yourself too. These are the stories and limiting beliefs that may be playing on a loop in your head and holding you back. We're going to work them until they suck no more.

Then the real fun begins. In Part 3, I unveil a framework of the ingredients you need to use authenticity as your new career secret weapon. I'll walk you through the Six Principles of Strategic Authenticity, anchored conveniently by an acronym HUMANS.

HUMILITY
UNEXPECTED
MODEL
ADAPT
NARRATE
SPARK

I'm going to give you so much more than words. We're going to walk through each principle. I'll connect you with stories and practical steps you can take to put these principles into practice immediately. I'll be sure you have a firm yet inspiring view of how to use the elements of HUMANS. And I'll give you a new mindset that will shift how you think, act, and succeed.

This might sound kinda insensitive, but this book isn't about making you a better person. I'm not coaching martyrs here. I'm going to teach you how to leverage the qualities you already have and show you how to expose them purposefully and strategically. And let me be clear: I am not giving you permission to simply "be." I'm going to give you the strategies to use your "be" to better connect, stand out, inspire, and succeed in your career.

Finally, in Part 4, we're going to talk about the bigger picture. I want to be sure you have everything you need to keep going well after you start using this book to paint your nails or eat your dinner on. I want you to understand the movement you can become a part of. Authenticity is a team sport. I need you on that team. And I promise that when you start experimenting with the authenticity principles, you'll inspire others to do the same. That's when the real fun begins.

You are unique. You are special. It's time to create your own path.

The matrix

One day, when I was a sophomore in college, my roommate came home from class all jacked up. She knew I was struggling to figure out my career since deciding that my initial path as a paper engineer was not my jam.

She said, "Erin, I found the career for you! It's high pay, low stress, and you just have to be good at math. And you're the only person I know that's good at math. It's called an actuary."

Being the bold, impressionable, IGW I was, I headed off to the library the very next day to research what this actuary thing was all about (yep, no Google then). I found a gray soft-cover 4x6-inch booklet that listed all the companies that hired actuaries, along with their addresses and contact information. I quickly realized there were a lot of actuaries in Connecticut, so I set my sights on an internship in the state.

After making several phone calls (this was also pre-email, and yes I'm a dinosaur), I finally swindled two companies into interviewing me. I told a white(ish) lie about already being out in Connecticut for Spring Break. The morning after my interviews, Aetna made me an offer to join their Actuarial Internship program that summer.

I was elated. I remember calling my parents to tell them. (I may also have told them a white(ish) lie about my trip to CT.) A few months later, I packed up my bags and moved my small Midwestern Michigan roots to the big bad city of Hartford, CT.

While much of that summer was fuzzy, there was a moment I'll never forget. One day all the actuarial interns completed a Myers-Briggs assessment. Once completed, about fifteen of us gathered in a hotel ballroom to receive the results. They put each of our names and results into a matrix and projected it up on the large screen. I noticed only one thing: I was all alone in my quadrant.

A few months later, they offered me a full-time job at Aetna as part of their formal actuarial program. I was rotated into a few different roles, all while I took the requisite actuarial exams. (The actuarial profession requires you to pass several really fucking hard graded-on-a-curve exams.) Over the next few years, I took five or six of these, and I was the recipient of five or six failing grades. There I sat, nine hundred plus miles from home, trudging down the wrong career path, still alone in a Myers-Briggs matrix.

Eventually I would realize though that my lonesome stance in a quadrant by myself was my superpower in disguise.

6 Authenticity is ishy

"Authenticity is about exposing who you are, when people least expect it."

~ Erin Hatzikostas - the super cool chick writing this book

You've likely been wondering about the "ish" in the book title. Maybe that little three letter extension is even the very thing that drew you in. There are two reasons I named the book *You Do You(ish)*. The first is that by making you curious, I'm demonstrating one key element of strategic authenticity (more on the elements later). But it's more than just a marketing ploy. The second reason is that it's actually an important distinction. While I'd love to think that authenticity is simply you doing you, the reality is *authenticity is about much more than simply being yourself.*

Like most people, you've probably subscribed to a simple definition of authenticity in your life until now. And that's okay. A lot of peace and freedom comes with a mantra that allows you an uninhibited right to be the person you are in this world. But when studied closely, authenticity is more nuanced than that. When we see someone who makes us almost involuntarily spew out, "Wow, they're so authentic," the traits they exhibit are deeper than an unrestrained version of who they are. And while I'm certainly not an etymologist-PhD-academic-type (I even had to Google "etymologist"), I do think it's pretty darn important that you fully understand the word's origin before we move on to the framework I've created to help you use authenticity in your work life.

A few years ago, I gave my first keynote speech on the concept of authenticity and its power in the workplace. I remember feeling all jazzed up after it was over, receiving several positive comments from people in the audience. But there was one comment that really stayed with me. A board member of a venture capital company had praise for the presentation but said he was stuck on one thing — how I defined authenticity.

I made a misstep in that presentation, which I won't repeat. I gave an overly precise formula for authenticity based solely on who I am. At that time, I'd come to the realization that authenticity was my secret weapon for success. But I hadn't spent enough time exploring its composition. Since that speech and that comment, I've become obsessed with finding and curating a richer and more accurate definition of authenticity. And more importantly, I've spent a lot of time thinking about what it means for others. I've also considered what it means in terms of the impact it can have on the workplace.

Authenticity is personal. It is inherently customizable. Yet, how in the hell do we know it when we see it? And so often, we *do* know it when we see it.

I decided to first explore the origin of the word. After sixteen years of marriage to a Greek American, I've learned that everything originates in Greece (or so the Greeks think, anyway). The word "authenticity" is derived from the word "authentikos," which means to be genuine, original, and authoritative. If you take the definition a bit further, it refers to someone who is worthy of acceptance, trust, belief, or reliability.

When I discovered this, I was happy to see that the word reflects an important juxtaposition. Authenticity is at an intersection of soft and hard, open and tough, humble and confident. I knew this intuitively because of the authenticity badge I had been pinned with. I knew that while I am a nice, approachable, and genuine person, I also can be quite direct and tough when needed. The Greeks clearly created this word for someone who was more than an open-book marshmallow.

Determining the definition helped to justify what I had always believed authenticity was *not*. It is not synonymous with transparency or just being. I often get asked if there is a risk of someone being too authentic at work. That almost always means they're thinking about someone being too *transparent*. Authenticity does not mean standing up at the next team meeting and saying, "So, last night after I got done making love to my spouse, I lay awake in bed worrying about our potential system collapse due to the lack of funds we have to do the necessary scalability upgrades."

authenticity ≠ transparency

Once you reorient your perception of authenticity to the definition and framework I'm going to walk you through rather than as a synonym of transparency, it'll become quite clear that you actually can't be too authentic.

If you're thinking, *WTF, Erin! You're telling me to be yin and yang? I'm so confused!*

More than anything, I simply want you to start by understanding that authenticity is

- not simply "being yourself"
- not a synonym for transparency
- personal
- something that, like with anything else, you simply practice doing one step at a time, day after day

Authenticity is about giving yourself permission to do the things that are sitting inside of you already. We're going to walk down the stairs to your soul's basement and check out all the stuff you've relegated to purgatory — the old vases you stacked carefully on dusty shelves because you never knew what to do with them; the boxed-up dumbbells you've always wanted to use but just haven't; and the picture frames you didn't quite have a spot for but didn't want to throw out. We're going to do this with your soul. We're going to take some of the stuff you find and send it to the dumpster. Some other stuff is going to get dusted off, repurposed, and used in a new way.

Authenticity is at the core of this book, and at first glance you might think this book preaches what so many others do. However, when most people talk about authenticity, they largely frame it as permission to be yourself.

I see it quite differently. I don't see authenticity as some passive, la-di-da free-Willy kinda thing. I have found that the real power comes not simply when you're *being* authentic. The real power comes when you start *doing* authentic. I realized that my career success skyrocketed when I made this slight adjustment … when I learned to *use* authenticity as my career secret weapon.

authenticity ≠ transparency

That small nuance changed everything. That small nuance is the heart of *You Do You(ish)*.

Strategic authenticity has the power to change your entire career. Strategic authenticity will allow you to hurl aside the crusty old career playbook you're sick of hearing and using (you know the one – it's dressed in shoulder pads, nylon stockings, and short feathered hair), the politics, the executive presence, the steak-dinner networking, the leaning-in, the martyrdom. Strategically using your authenticity will give you the modern-day career playbook that I know you need and deserve.

Get ready to get selfish, my friend. It's the best thing you can do for yourself *and* for others.

7 Data for the doubters

*"There are two types of people in the world:
those who can extrapolate from incomplete data sets."*

~ Leandro Herrero - speaker and author
And about the quote ... wait for it to hit you, it will

Okay, so far I've talked about how I hate (most) books, love authenticity, and believe that authenticity can be your new modern-day secret weapon to get you up and over the walls you're facing in your career. I hope I've convinced you that authenticity isn't just some hippie-lovefest concept, but a powerful quality that you don't just fall into. It's a state of not just being, but of acting.

But is being more authentic just a woobie blanket that helps you get through the work BS more easily? Or will it actually lead to tangible results?

I was a statistics major in college. Yes, really. I have no frickin' idea how I skated out of an institution with that degree, because these days I struggle with my children's elementary school math. (I admit to just recently Googling "What is a polygon?") And while I'm not a complete poser, I'm now much more of a big-picture kinda person. I love reading between the lines to draw a conclusion that might take a more academic type twenty years of data surfing to come to the same conclusion. I also prefer to rely on really smart people at institutions like, say, Harvard, to do the data work. So to prove (with cold hard facts) that authenticity can make a tangible impact, I'm going to link together three highly credible studies that I think make the business case that *authenticity = results.*

FACT #1

Trust. One of my favorite Harvard Business Review papers is called "The Neuroscience of Trust"[3] by Paul J. Zak. In this study, the author and his team found that trust was one of the most critical factors in differentiating high-performing organizations. Not only were people much happier at work when trust was present, they performed better and thus yielded better results for the company.

The team spent over ten years studying the effects of trust on organizations. The foundation of their work was based on a conclusion drawn from others' work with rodents, which found that when rats trusted other rats, they released higher levels of oxytocin in their brains. The Harvard team set out to test if the same was true in humans. They assumed that if they could prove that humans also released oxytocin when they trusted someone, they could test if organizations with higher trust performed differently than those with lower trust. (Now do you see why I leave this hard part to the academics? The IGW in me could never wait ten years to find out the answer to one question!)

The Harvard team set up an experiment where two strangers were paired together and, of course, they had no idea what the actual experiment was about. Person A was given the opportunity to choose an amount of money to send to Person B, via a computer. If Person A decided to keep the money instead, they could. If they decided to send the money to Person B, the money would triple. However, here was the catch: Person B could decide to either keep all of the money or they could choose to share some portion (or all of it) back to Person A. This wasn't your average amateur experiment; prior to this money-exchange thing, they drew blood from each participant so they could measure the levels of oxytocin in each.

As the experiment unfolded, the researchers confirmed the results were consistent with what had been seen in rats – higher oxytocin levels correlated with higher levels of trust. Specifically, the higher the oxytocin level in Person A, the more money they chose to send to Person B, indicating they had higher trust that Person B would share money back with them. They also found the same to be true in the other direction. When Person B's oxytocin levels were higher, they shared more money back with Person A.

Put simply, this work confirmed that a) higher levels of oxytocin in humans directly correlates with a person's level of trust with another person, and b) researchers are a little insane as they go to incredible extremes to prove their point.

Okay, take a deep breath here. We have to take this one step further. From this blood-drawing mafia-like experiment, the team then applied these findings more broadly to companies. They wanted to prove that levels of trust correlated with tangible differences in culture and outcomes within the work setting. They found a host of suckers who were willing to have their blood drawn and oxytocin (trust) measured in order to draw conclusions about key behaviors of those exhibiting higher levels of trust. Conclusions were extrapolated and applied to several thousand companies to compare the results across a number of work-related metrics, including stress-levels, productivity, and employee engagement.

Phew!

Ready for this? Harvard's research found that companies with higher levels of trust have 74% less stress, 50% higher productivity, and 76% higher employee engagement. (Again, engagement = people giving a shit about their job.) These numbers are no joke. There is a compelling competitive advantage if a company can have employees walking around trusting one another.

FACT #2

Now that we know oxytocin and trust are related, what kicks our oxytocin into high gear so we can increase trust in the workplace? And what's missing in people and interactions that sends our oxytocin plummeting?

In another unrelated Harvard Business Review study[4], which is also the basis of a TED Talk ("How to build (and rebuild) trust" by Frances Frei), Frei and her colleague Anne Morriss dissect a formula for trust. Now, Frei and Morriss seem to be a little more my style. Instead of drawing blood from animals and humans for, like, a decade, they sought the answers based on what they had observed after many years working within organizations to help shape their leaders' skills.

The authors conclude that there are three primary components of trust: empathy, logic, and authenticity. They call this the Trust Triangle. They explain that it can be thought of as a three-legged stool, and if any of these three components are "wobbly," that affects how much you'll be trusted or have trust in others. Trust isn't set in stone. Trust changes depending on your levels of empathy, logic, and authenticity.

Let's look at empathy first. Others are seen as trustworthy if you also perceive that they care about you – your feelings, your well-being, your success. The second component is logic. This is how credible and accurate you are when you say something. Are the things you say based on sound judgement, facts, and knowledge? In other words: Are you just making shit up or do you seem to form your thoughts based on a reasonable set of data? Frei and Morriss define the third component, authenticity, as *people experiencing the "real you."* Essentially what they're saying is that you need to be seen as someone who cares about others (empathy), is sane and credible (logic), and is being the real you (authenticity).

Now, I love this … and I disagree slightly.

I think that if Frei and Morriss took a closer look at the root of the concept of authenticity, they would see that logic and empathy are subcomponents of authenticity. In our earlier Greek lesson, I wrote that "authentikos" is defined as genuine, original, and authoritative. Based on that, I'd give authenticity a solid 75% credit for being the driver of trust. (Warning: This is my typical fuzzy math and likely why I failed at my first career as an actuary.)

The conclusion thus far? People are way more likely to give a shit about their work (be engaged) when they trust someone. And people are much more likely to trust someone who is authentic.

As a reminder, we set off on this journey to prove that authenticity = results. So, now let's take a closer look at the impact that a more engaged workforce has on results.

FACT #3

This one's easy. We're going to leave our friends at Harvard and instead look at some data from Gallup. Every year, Gallup conducts a well-regarded Employee Engagement survey. In the 2017 study[5], Gallup found that companies with higher engagement were 21% more profitable. And this isn't rocket science, right? If you care more about your work, you're going to be more productive, more innovative, and more collaborative. Multiply that by hundreds or thousands, and no doubt that's going to affect all metrics of a company's performance, including how much money it makes.

Pulling all this together, when people see more authenticity in the workplace, they trust the organization and its leaders more. And when they trust people more, they are more engaged in their work. And when they're more engaged, they make more moola for the company (and likely themselves too!). Said another way:

authenticity = trust

trust = engagement

engagement = money

Therefore: authenticity = money.

BONUS FACT

If all this data talk made your eyes cross, here's one last fact: Oprah. Oprah once said, "I had no idea that being your authentic self could make me as rich as I've become. If I had, I'd have done it a lot earlier."

Mic drop.

8

My ground zero

"We've got a responsibility to live up to the legacy of those who came before us by doing all that we can to help those who come after us."

~ Michelle Obama - attorney, author, former US First Lady, and authentic to the core

One of the things I often get asked is, "Why do you think there's such a lack of authenticity in the workplace?" From my perspective, it's a simple answer. We emulate those before us.

We've been caught in a vortex we don't control, emulating a slightly altered version of some dude's success formula from forty years ago. I'm sure there was a time when being more rigid, more pretentious, and more plastic served someone well. And then others started to copy the formula. It's a natural tendency. We've been doing it since we were babies, as we learned to walk, talk, and everything else.

But the formula gets reinforced over and over again. Boss after boss. Or by the hundreds of leadership consultants that have made darn good businesses out of putting formulas to what drove success before. Sprinkle on top of that some healthy doses of fear, ego, and selfishness, and it's no surprise Corporate America is caught in a vicious cycle of same shit, different decade.

One thing can turn this all around, help us all get out of the cycle we're spinning in. That one thing is seeing other people being successful doing things authentically.

It happened nearly every day of my childhood, Monday through Friday. My dad would sit at the kitchen counter telling stories about his workday.

Now, both my parents were teachers. My mom — sweet, patient, and perfect in all ways — was the quintessential elementary school teacher. (I am not my mom.)

My father, on the other hand, is a bit more direct, impatient, and unique. Over his twenty-five-plus years teaching, he taught everything from industrial arts to math. He also was a guidance counselor and athletic director.

My dad's life is composed of a constant stream of stories, many of which he tells and re-tells on a regular basis. Every day he would come home from school and sit at the counter to recall his day to my mother while she prepared dinner. He'd belly-up to the kitchen counter, open his Heineken, and talk about the day's shenanigans.

One of my favorites went something like this:

"Today in math class I walked in and set down a tape recorder. I wrote on the blackboard, I'm a ______, I'm a ______, I'm a ______, I'm a ______, I'm a ______ *and walked out of the room. The kids looked around at each other like they'd just entered outer space. A few seconds went by and on came the beautiful voice of James Taylor.*

Well, I'm a steamroller, baby

I'm 'bout to roll all over you

Yes, I'm a steamroller, baby

I'm 'bout to roll all over you ...

The students listened to the song in complete puzzlement. And then, a few started to get it. And then a few more. The first answer to this pop quiz was ... 'steamroller.' Do you know what those other three answers are? Cement mixer, demolition derby, and napalm bomb."

My father had been having some issues with kids listening in class. Instead of taking the standard approach and yelling at the kids or handing out punishments, this was his way of grabbing their attention, teaching them a lesson, and having some fun while doing it.

His approach hit on several of the Six Principles of Strategic Authenticity that I'll go into later. It was *unexpected*, it used *narration*, and in the end, his approach *sparked* the class to change rather than forcing them to change.

My dad told stories like this nearly every day. There was always some new, authentic way he would approach a lesson or deal with a situation. He was rarely "normal."

My dad had an incredible teaching career; he was beloved, he made an impact, and he loved his job. In fact, he still has "kids" contact him decades later to tell him about a story they remember or something he said that inspires them still. Do they remember how to figure out if a triangle is acute, obtuse, or isosceles? Probably not. But they remember his stories, the jokes, and his character – the authenticity.

The same is true at home. I've forgotten many details of my childhood. I don't remember how often my dad played with me. I don't have any recollection of how many basketball practices he drove me to. I don't remember if he ever chose work over me. But I remember the most important thing:

You can be authentic and have success. In fact, being authentic fuels success.

I've always known much of my personality was handed down from my father. However, it took me about forty years to realize, it wasn't just his DNA that made me who I am. It was the way he demonstrated time and time again that it's okay to do things differently at work. It's okay to be funny, unorthodox, and unexpected. Most importantly, it wasn't just acceptable; it drove success.

I hope I can be a beacon for you like my dad was for me. I hope you see that I'm not just here to say it's "okay" to be authentic. I'm here to show you that being and *doing* authentic will get you amazing results. My career success wasn't an accident. My leading a company through a massive turnaround wasn't an accident. My success in my new business isn't an accident. My authenticity continues to help me — and those around me — win.

You're not lacking anything that will stop you from having the same success I've had. You are special in your own way. Perhaps you help others. Or you're trusted to get shit done. Or you're given messy things and make magic. If you sprinkle your authenticity on top of the luscious donut that you already are, people will eat you up. There are opportunities and successes coming your way that you can't even begin to imagine.

It's time to stop thinking of yourself as doing "good enough." Good enough is for people content watching talk shows all day. Good enough is for people who worked half as hard as you at work yesterday. Good enough is for the birds. You, my friend, are meant to be fucking notorious.

None of this notoriousness stops at *you* either. I don't want you to be the one shining light in a sea of assholes. I'm confident that if you practice what I preach in this book and you share your authentic successes with others, you'll no longer be sparkling in a dirty-ass ocean, you'll be swimming in a brightly lit infinity pool.

An authenticity movement lights tiny fires everywhere.

That movement starts here.

9

The power of a yawn

"Energy is contagious:
either you affect people,
or you infect people."

~ T. Harv Eker - author, speaker, and businessman

We're almost done with setting a solid foundation for the power of authenticity. If I've already convinced you that authenticity is the superpower you need, then yay you!

But I want you to be so insanely aligned with this concept that when you think someone is going to look at you like you have two heads for doing something authentically, you'll trudge forward anyway. 'Cause trust me … you're going to start down this path of being your authentic badass self and then have moments of doubt. Worry will creep in. Concern that other people will think you're a bit kooky. If you're truly going to grasp these concepts and sustain your authenticity-first strategy, I want to be sure you're 100% convinced this is the right path. Here's the last thing you need to know:

Authenticity is as contagious as a yawn in church.

You know the feeling. You had no clue you were even tired. And then you see someone yawn. It's like a centrifugal force. You yawn too. Authenticity does the same thing.

My first authenticity "yawn" in the workplace came from my boss, Martha Temple. When I worked for Martha, she was the head of Aetna's international division and the person who hired me into my first "big girl" job. Martha wasn't a typical executive. First of all, she was an actuary, but she clearly evaded the stereotype (i.e., she had a personality). She also wasn't afraid to wear her flaws on her sleeves. I have so many Martha stories, but one of my favorites was the time when she and I were in London for a series of meetings. We had dinner one evening with a potential business partner, and they took us out to a Japanese restaurant. I distinctly remember sitting down next to Martha and her looking over at me and saying, "Huh, the Japanese eat with chopsticks too?"

This would have been funny for anyone to say, but she was the head of an international company, and that made it hysterical. Martha never put on a front that she was any smarter or more cultured than she really was. Martha was authentic through and through.

Unfortunately, many people don't have this force in their life. Especially in their work life. No one has started the authenticity spin for them. But guess what? Authenticity doesn't have to be spun by some Grand Poobah. YOU can start things spinning. For you and for others. Including those above you.

When people see someone exhibiting authenticity, they can't resist being inspired. It's the most contagious leadership trait I know. It's not like you're thinking, *Ah, man, look at Sally go. She's leading with such discipline and rigor. I really should get my shit together and do that.* Nope, that's not how authenticity works. Instead, when you see Sally in action, you think, *Ah, that is so refreshing and simple. I should do that too.*

Let me give you a real-life example. One day I was getting ready for a short vacation. I was taking a Friday off so we could enjoy a long weekend up in Vermont. Like I'm sure you do, I was racing around trying to tie up loose ends the evening beforehand. I had almost logged off my computer when I caught myself. I'd forgotten to write my OOO message (out of office). I sat down to update the boring language I still had sitting in there from my last getaway: *I am currently out of the office, returning on xx date. I will check in when I can, however if you need anything urgently, please contact so-and-so.*

Then I thought, *This sucks! Am I a robot?!* I'd been writing some version of that same god-awful Obligatory Oblivious Outage message for the last twenty years. Who had I become? I took another look at it. *This message is going out to hundreds of people, and I'm missing a huge opportunity to inspire them!*

In just a few minutes, I rewrote that message to say, Hey there. I'm taking a much-needed long weekend for some R&R with my family up in Vermont. I won't be checking in, but if something happens and things are about to blow up, contact so-and-so.

While I never got a direct response to my message from anyone, I immediately noticed something. Over the next few weeks, I was getting OOOs that were different. There were more human ones popping up every day. There were OOOs that gave people permission to actually be OOO. I knew it wasn't a coincidence. I knew that my tiny authentic experiment had spread like wildfire. So, I wondered, *If that spread so fast, what else can I ignite?*

I know you've had these urges. Those times when either you thought of doing something differently or you saw a commercial that sparked an idea in you. Maybe it was something you read. Or maybe it was the tiny rebel that lives inside you that simply wanted to be more authentic. What if instead of holding back, you treated this like a fun experiment? And not an experiment about results – one focused on simply observing how others around you respond. Do they smile? Do they get curious? Do they start to emulate you? Too often we think about these unique and bold moves as if we're stepping into concrete that's just about to set. Like if you step where you're not supposed to, you might get stuck, laughed at, and leave a permanent mark. The reality is that life – and living it authentically – is a constant experiment that creates a path, using one small pebble at a time. It's always changing. It's never permanent. And it can be reshaped infinitely.

Every authentic move you make, however small, moves you forward and inspires others. It triggers something positive in those around you — your employee, your peer, your boss, your spouse, your child, a connection on LinkedIn, the grocery store clerk, your mother, your daughter's soccer coach.

Everyone can spread authenticity. Let's do just that.

I really want the job. But...

It was a Friday afternoon, and I was working from home. I was in that glide-into-the-weekend mode, not working on anything that would hurt my brain too much, when my boss texted me: *Can we talk?*

[inhale … exhale]

Then he called. "This is pretty heavy for a Friday, but I've decided to leave the company. I want to know if it's okay for me to recommend you as our next COO."

I paused.

"Uh, no thank you."

While I always had ambition, this role felt like the tipping point — it would tip my career-life teeter-totter in the wrong direction. I quickly whipped out my Compromise Calculator and thought, *Nope. If I go for this bigger job, I'll have to compromise my family, my health, maybe even my soul. I'm good where I'm at.*

But it was Friday, and although I did say no, I asked to think about it over the weekend. I sought other people's feedback – friends, family. Feedback was mixed. But I distinctly recall telling the dad of one of my daughter's friends about it when he brought his daughter over for a playdate. "Oh, yeah, you'd have to give up so much time with your family. It'd be a lot of stress…blah blah blah…" Not one hint of *you should go for it.*

I gave myself time to sit with my own thoughts. I realized I was worried about becoming the people and having the life of those executives before me. And then it hit me like a freight train to my big-ass forehead: *You shouldn't* not *do something because you hate the way it was done before.*

I came back on Monday and said yes to the job. But now I had to figure out just how to do it my own way.

PART 2

Who Says That's Your Playlist?

10

Stop, primer time

(It helps to put in a little MC Hammer here.)

"If you run into an asshole in the morning,
you ran into an asshole.
If you run into assholes all day,
you're the asshole."

~ Raylan Givens in *Justified* -
and one of my father's favorite quotes

Now that you're bought in and are excited and pumped up ...

Now that you're ready to embrace authenticity as your new secret weapon ...

Now that you want to give me a huge hug to thank me for showing you the light ...

I'm going to piss you off.

Instead of marching you right to the Holy Grail — the HOW of diving deep into authenticity so you can start using it to change your career — I have to do something else first. You see, what would go down if we all succumbed to our IGW-ness* is that you'd read the book, pump your fists in the air, and run out to conquer the world. And that would be great, until you ran into an asshole.

** Reminder: IGW = Instant Gratification Whore. I know, it's dirty. But spot-on, right?*

While it could be any one of the plethora of assholes that are swimming around your workplace fishbowl right now, it's more likely that the first asshole you'll run into is … you.

Let's be honest. We often treat ourselves much worse than we treat others.

How many times have you been on the phone with your friend, talking them through their big issue, and you can see clear as day: They are so much better than they think they are. You coach them and caress them and calm them. You light the flame they desperately need lit to get out of whatever mess they're in. Then you hang up, and I'd be willing to guess that less than twelve hours later, you succumb to some shitty-ass situation you're in, all the while telling yourself, *there's not much I can do. I guess I deserve this. I'm not as good as that person.* Blah-diddy-blah.

So, what we must first do – and I do this with nearly all my clients – is recognize the Sucky Songs we're singing to ourselves. We must see them, write them down, burn them, and rewrite them. To mix metaphors here just for kicks – we can't haul an old dresser up from the basement and just start painting that thing. First, we've gotta sand it down, prime it, and ready it for change. Then and only then will the new paint stick. That's what we're going to do here in Part 2. We're going to get you ready so your authenticity playbook will stick (the metaphor is getting really messy, I know). And then, my friend, when we head into Part 3 and dive fully into what strategic authenticity looks, feels, and acts like, you'll be ready to crush it. Not just for a day or two, but for a lifetime.

11

Let's get metaphysical, metaphysical. I wanna get metaphysical ...

(It helps to channel Olivia Newton-John on this one.)

"The problem is not the problem.
The problem is your attitude about the problem."

~ Jack Sparrow in *The Pirates of the Caribbean*

Mindsetty stuff isn't something I've been practicing or preaching my whole life. In fact, the realization that our brains are more than a repository for all the shit we've learned is a fairly recent revelation for me. I've always appreciated my mind. I love to learn. In fact, I love to learn so much that I kamikazed out of a perfectly amazing, high-paying job in large part because I always want to be learning.

But mindset is a whole different ball game ... in a totally different ball universe. The notion that our minds actually create the matter — the stuff, experiences, feelings, success — in our lives, has been a slow-build to epiphany for me since I left the corporate world. Why? Well, for one, I had more space. I was no longer in the black hole of back-to-back meetings, PowerPoint decks, and corporate trainings. Mindset also became more critical than ever in the place where I landed. Entrepreneurship is a risk. It's hard. It definitely doesn't bring overnight success. And it took me only a little bit of time wandering in this world before I started hearing about the importance of mindset. So, I started on a journey to strengthen a part of my brain I had left largely abandoned for much of my life.

One of the most profound experts in the world of "mind over matter" is Joe Dispenza. I first heard Joe on *The goop Podcast*. I admit, I only half paid attention to the first ten minutes. When I started listening, his concepts sounded too complicated and woo-woo for me, but just as I started to zone out, something he said hit me like a freight train. He started to give example after example of people who were sick, many with critical or chronic illnesses, who overcame their maladies just by changing their mindset.

This is when I sat up, rewound the podcast to the beginning, and started listening all over again. And here's the layman's summary of what I learned: It's largely not genes that create disease; 99% of illness is created by lifestyle and behavior. And when we focus on the present (which is built on the past), we hardwire the environment around us. If we instead focus on creating a new wiring system in our brains, we begin building a new environment around ourselves ... a new future. I thought: *If people can do this and cure their disease, people can certainly do this to cure their career.*

Now, let's jump out of the deep and complex world of Joe Dispenza and back into our *You Do You(ish)*, simple(ish) world. What this means is that if you often tune into some crappy AM station where they keep playing a Sucky Song, like "Guess I'm Dumb" by Glen Campbell, then you're probably going to be singing this song over and over in your head, even when you don't realize it. And pretty soon you won't just be singing it, you'll be living it.

Instead, if you spend more time tuning into some hell-yes FM station, it's likely that you start singing Suck-cess Songs. Then what's happening to you starts looking a lot more like Sia jamming out to "Unstoppable" on stage. And where are these radio stations … uh, stationed? Of course, in your head. Your own mind is responsible for creating the frequency and the playlist that dictates your day, your week, your life.

If we're going to pave the way for you to be the most authentic, kickass, best version of yourself, we first have to change what songs are playing in your head.

If you're going to let me take you further on this quest for badassery, balance, and a career without compromise or selling out, you have to promise me that you will first travel inward to become aware of the Sucky Songs you may be playing over and over inside your head. For some of you, we're going to work together to move the dial a bit to the right or a bit to the left. For others (you know who you are), we're going to get out a toolbox of fine-tuning equipment and get you jammin' to a whole new playlist.

I'm going to walk through the five top hits that I've heard played by the hundreds of people I've coached and mentored over the years. Some — or maybe all — of these may sound familiar to you. You might even have some of your own Sucky Songs. The goal here is to expose these suckers, delete them, and then start building a whole new playlist.

12

Sucky Song #1: I have to compromise my family for my career

"Will you read my book?"
"If you let me, with all the swears I know are in it."

~ Me and my 9-year-old son

You want to be a great parent. It sits at the top of your life to-do list. And as such, there is no higher priority than knowing you've done all you can for your children. You may also have convinced yourself that time is the most significant measure of quality on your "being a great parent" rubric.

You've said it more than once: *I'm good where I'm at in my career. I value balance over climbing the corporate ladder.*

I'm asking you to consider this a Sucky Song. I want you to stop singing this song because it's limiting your access to success and fulfillment. If you'll trust me, we can rewrite it together. I still want you to be a class A, number 1 parent. I'm not asking you to rethink your parenting goals. I'm asking you to rethink your parenting role. Stop judging your success as a parent by how much you *do* for your children and start judging it by how much you *live* for your children.

Have you been to a high school graduation recently? Well, it doesn't even matter. Most speeches have been saying the same thing for the past century:

- Follow your dreams.
- Be bold.
- Take risks.
- Dream big.
- The sky's the limit.
- Make change.

Why do we wait until our children are eighteen years old to give them this message?! Why can't we give them this message earlier in life? And better still, why don't we *show* them what they can be and how they can live a full life?

Of course, if you're going to become a parent, you should want to be the best on the planet. The most impactful way to do this isn't to suffocate them by being there all the time, picking them up as soon as they hit the ground, and being in the front row of every concert or sporting event. The best way to give your children the ultimate life is to demonstrate what they can dream of having and being.

Great parents don't suffocate, they demonstrate.

Let me tell you a story.

I traveled to Omaha to spend a few days focused on leadership development, and my team had just finished an all-day leadership meeting. We were sitting at dinner when my husband sent me a text: *Ella applied for student council today. Here's her application.*

My daughter was nine years old and this was the first year of student council. I knew she was interested in putting her name in, but I had forgotten all about it. I had no direct hand in her application (and neither did my husband). As I pulled up the picture from the text and read it, my jaw dropped. Her response to the last question left me gaping at my phone.

Application question: "What do you think are the most important qualities of a leader?"

Ella's response: "To be kind to others, to help others, and to be ready for anything."

I scanned the table and the faces of those seated near me. We had just spent hours working on our own leadership skills. I knew we could spend another two weeks and not be able to articulate a more succinct and powerful definition of leadership.

I'd never said these exact words to my daughter. I'd never coached Ella on the qualities of a leader. I was not physically there when she had to complete her application. But …

Ella had been in the car many times while I was on a call. Ella came into my office often and watched me leading people as the CEO of a large company. Ella watched me and her father debate who would stay home when one of them was too sick to go to school. She saw time and time again that it is possible to be a girl and be a boss.

We tend to think that success is primarily determined by what you learn, when in fact,

Success is driven 10% by what you *learn* and 90% by what you *see.*

About a year ago I was planning the logistics of speaking at a day-long conference when I realized the kids wouldn't have school that day, and we had no daycare options. Well, the old Erin would have freaked out. But now that authenticity is my number-one career playbook, it didn't take me long to decide, *I'll just take them with me.*

I asked the kids if they wanted to go, and I told them we could even make a fun trip out of it and stay at the hotel the night before. They almost lost their minds with excitement. A road trip to a hotel with a pool?! I mean, there aren't many things more exciting than that for an eleven- and eight-year-old. We had a great time. We had dinner and watched football at the hotel restaurant. They swam in the pool. And they came to the conference with me the next day. The organizers even made name tags for them! When I got to the part in my presentation that talked about the value of including your children, we orchestrated a semi-dramatic kid run-down from the back of the room!

And you know what? My talk was pretty darn good, but what more than 90% of the people probably remember is that I *demonstrated* what I talked about. The inspiration and good feels that working moms and dads (and probably others too) got from seeing my kids at the event trumped anything I actually said that day.

I'd like to challenge you to start thinking about how you can integrate your homelife into your work life. Stop beating yourself up about how much time you spend on your job and, by conclusion, how much less time you spend with your children. Don't make it a zero-sum game. If you start to recognize that what you do for work can and should make a direct impact on the growth and future of your children, everything changes.

Bring your children to your workplace. When you're on a call, invite them to listen. When you're putting together a presentation, ask them to be your test audience (and be sure to ask for feedback – their feedback is gold). When you travel to a conference, consider bringing them along. When you're stressed about how to juggle work and homelife, ask them their opinion. Include them in decisions. Share your success and your failures. Take jobs that fill you with joy; leave those that don't. Demonstrate.

Spend less time speaking the words you want your kids to hear and more time demonstrating the life you want your kids to live.

What do you think? Are you ready to get rid of the "Compromise Family for Career" Sucky Song? If you're mostly there, tuck it far away in your attic with all your other old dusty CDs. Or if you're like, "Fuck yes!" I'm over it, feel free to burn that shit, very safely, in a firepit out back (unless you're in California or Oregon, in which case please just put it in the trash).

I'd love to hear what new song you write. Post your new Suck-cess Song title on Instagram with #suckcesssong and tag me too @erinhatzikostas. I can't wait to hear it!

Spend less time
speaking the words
you want your kids
to hear
and more time
demonstrating the
life you want your
kids to live.

13

Sucky Song #2: I'm not qualified for the job

"It had long since come to my attention that people of accomplishment rarely sat back and let things happen to them. They went out and happened to things."

~ Leonardo da Vinci - painter and jack of many other trades, none of which I'm guessing he had the experience to do when he first started doing them

My first big break into the corporate Big League came via an offer to lead strategy and business development for the international division of Aetna. I was in my late twenties, and after failing in the actuarial field, I had taken on various roles within the company and been a solid designated hitter. I was the kind of person who raised their hand high every time there was a new off-the-side-of-your-desk, highly ill-defined project, and that had helped me get noticed and easily land a place in the lineup on several new teams.

And then one day they drafted me to be a project manager in

a small(ish) division of our company. This was my first role with a seat at the table; I reported directly to the division president and was part of the leadership team.

Pretty quickly, my boss started to give me more and more responsibility. First it was to manage the product team (two very eclectic older men and a long list of projects). Next it was the strategic planning responsibility.

A few years into the role, the CEO of Aetna was pushing us to expand significantly. We needed to grow into a legit international healthcare company. And we needed someone to lead that expansion. I remember the day my boss asked me if I wanted to be that person. I laughed. (Probably out loud.) Me? I had no frickin' clue how to do something like this. I wasn't a fit for any role with "international" in the title. I was just under thirty, a small-town girl from Northern Michigan, and I'd traveled out of the country only a few times. I spoke only English, though I counted among my myriad talents managing, "I'll have a beer, please" in three other languages. Long story short: I felt soooo unqualified for the job.

The Sucky Song playing in my head was from a station that was home to many of my longtime earworms: *I don't have the experience it takes to do this job.* I know you've also belted this one out in the car on the way to work more than a few times yourself.

Trust me, I can sing, hear, and see the lyrics of the song you may run on a loop in your head ...

They won't value me.
They won't understand me.
I don't matter.
I don't have enough to offer.
Chorus (repeat): I won't live up to their expectations.

These are the exact words I've been told by people just like you over the years.

If you're thinking or singing this song, you need a Song Replacement Plan. And rewriting the lyrics to this Sucky Song is easier than you think. I want you to replace your "I can't" statements with "What if" questions:

What if I don't take on the new opportunity? Who would take it instead?

What if I take it and I mess up? What's the worst thing that could happen?

What if I don't take it? Will I be doing some of the work anyway?

What if I take it and do it differently than the person before me?

Answer these and you've got the building blocks to your new song. You'll have started to change the melody that has been playing on auto-loop in your head. You'll turn that sad (likely country) song into something with a better beat, a new vibe, new possibilities.

Successful people don't say: "I can't." Successful people say: "What if?"

As I contemplated taking my first major league role and leading our international expansion, I found that the most powerful "What if" question I asked myself was *What if I DON'T take the job?*

And here's what I came up with: They'll probably go out and hire some middle-aged white dude who has tons of buzzwords on his resumé. He'd stroll into the organization like a savior, meanwhile not knowing shit about what we do. For the first few months, leadership would sit awestruck, hanging on his every word. But as time went on, it would become clear that he doesn't know a thing about international healthcare (at the time, pretty much no one in the world did), and he would spend two years running around fucking things up.

Now, I recognized the inner cynic talking through me, but it was the new Suck-cess Song I needed to sing to move the other self-doubting song out of the way. And that my friend, is totally fair game!

One of my favorite podcasts is *The Life Coach School* hosted by Brooke Castillo. In one episode she talks about how people feel like they lack confidence but they can't understand it, because while they have big-balls confidence in some areas, in others (typically work), they pull back. She explains that often it's actually not a lack of confidence; rather, it's a lack of tolerance for failure that holds people back.

Does this resonate with you?

Is the difference between you having gigantic success and just being okay with "good enough" largely based on your unwillingness to face that you might fail? I can't answer that for you, but I want you to ask yourself this question … and continue to ask this question on a regular basis.

Consider what song you sing when *someone else* makes a mistake. What plays in your head? Then think of a time where a company or person you were working with screwed up on something and then recovered rock star-style. Did you have a greater appreciation for them after they made a mistake and recovered?

Is your
unwillingness
to fail
holding you back?

A friend of mine regularly orders nutritional supplements from 1st Phorm. One day she received an email from them after a manufacturing issue created a shipping backlog of one of their primary products. Instead of hiding it or sending a stuffy note apologizing, 1st Phorm used it as an opportunity to authentically connect with their customers.

One of the leaders at the company shot a video that shows him in the front office, and the camera quickly pans to show that the normally filled cubicles are empty. He then walks to the warehouse in the back where people are working on packaging their product. He even shows the president of the company sitting at a table, working alongside the other employees. He goes on to say that they had an issue with their coolers and it set them back. He talks about how they are a company focused on quality, saying that they weren't willing to cut corners. He explains that this was the reason for the backlog. Not only was this video done in a way that showed genuine authenticity, it was also unique, so I've now shared it with several of the people I coach to inspire them to turn a mistake into an opportunity to connect.

I love this example, especially because it was not my own experience. The way 1st Phorm recovered from their mistake was so impactful to my friend (and in her words, "a great example of authenticity") that she shared the communication and video with me (and possibly others).

Here's the thing …

If you go through life without making mistakes, you're sure to blend in.

This is true for a person. This is true for a company. And the last thing any of us want to do is blend in. Am I right? Instead, let's rewrite your "I'm not good enough" Sucky Song to a Suck-cess Song that is more like "Without mistakes you run the risk of looking like everyone else."

It may not be something Taylor Swift would make a hit song into, but it's true. I want you to see that taking risks inevitably comes with accepting mistakes. And those mistakes can be opportunities to create fans. If you can experiment with that, the flywheel will start turning and turning.

You take more risks,
you make a few mistakes,
you recover like a rock star,
people love you,
you become more confident.
Rinse and repeat.

Hmm ... I might be onto something

About thirty hot seconds after I was appointed COO, I had to lead a critical make-it-or-break-it contract negotiation, and I had no frickin' clue what to do.

I remember the day we sat down to kick off negotiations. It was just me and a senior executive from the other company. He was your typical looking "man of corporate success." White, in his fifties, a shade of gray in his hair, and the glasses. Despite my pettiness here, he was a good guy. But I also assumed he had been in this kind of quagmire about thirty times more than I had.

In my typical, Type A fashion, I remember semi-unconsciously asking him, "So, what's important to you in this negotiation?" I'm pretty sure I caught him off guard because he kinda spilled his guts and helped me immediately understand what was most important to him in the negotiation. Naturally, he then turned the question back on me.

When out of my mouth I puked up, "Well, our financials are struggling. And if I can negotiate this deal without a price increase, I'll have a good shot at become the next CEOoooo. And I kinda want to become the next CEOoooo." I remember thinking, What the fuck, Erin! Why can't you learn to just keep some shit in?!

He didn't laugh. He didn't roll his eyes. He said, "Well, let me try and help you do that."

Several months later, and through one hell of a gun-match negotiation between our lawyers and procurement overlords, we got the deal done. And not only did the other company not increase our rates, we ended up with a contract that lowered our rates.

It was in that moment that I realized being authentic isn't just something to help me stay "me." I could actually use authenticity as my secret career weapon.

Don't just be authentic. Do authentic.

14

Sucky Song #3: Others have more money; that's why they can do it

"The day that you plant the seed is not the day you eat the fruit."

~ Fabienne Fredrickson - founder of Boldheart and a cool chick I found on the internet

I want you to pause and think about the last time you were in a meeting with a manager, senior executive, or even an entrepreneur and secretly felt jealous that they had that role and you didn't. You knew it wasn't that they were smarter than you. It was just that they had it easier, right? Or so you thought.

You might say to yourself, *I could do that job, but I can't afford the support they have at home (childcare, cleaning services, etc.) to take care of my children and my house.* Or maybe, *I have kids to put through college. I can't take the financial risk they took to get here.* You could even be thinking, *I'm sure they come from a long line of money and success. Must be nice.*

I get it. But let me help you rewrite this song too.

On a blah weekend in April, I had nothing planned and I was on the hunt for something to keep the kids, then six and four years old, moving and entertained. We decided to go on a road trip to "the city," which for us is New Haven, Connecticut. New Haven is about an hour's drive from us, and it's nowhere near being a big city. With a population of about 130,000 contained within just twenty square miles, most people have heard of New Haven for only two reasons: Yale and pizza. New Haven is also the home of my podcast co-host, Nicole Licata Grant. I call Nicole the unofficial mayor of New Haven. If you want to learn about New Haven from a Townie Gownie (as she calls herself), who is also a Yale graduate, and be both intellectually stimulated and pee your pants from laughing so hard at the same time, I highly recommend listening to our *b Cause with Erin & Nicole* podcast. (How's that for integrated marketing?!)

The kids and I decided to go visit Nicole. This was well before she and I decided to become joined at the hip to co-host our podcast. Nicole and I met when we were both just beginning our ventures into the adult world. I was an aspiring actuary (fail) and Nicole was working where many confused Ivy League grads first land — at a major consulting firm (also a fail). We found ourselves at the same Halloween party. Nicole rolled in as Boogie Nights' Roller Girl (skates and all), and I was dressed as some sort of lame athlete. We knew immediately that we had to become friends. We never could have predicted that twenty years later, we'd be hosting a podcast together. (We couldn't have predicted podcasts would exist either.)

Back to the story.

While we were driving, the kids started asking a bunch of questions about Nicole. I explained that she recently moved back to New Haven after living in Washington, DC for several years. I also explained that she was divorced and had a boyfriend. When the kids probed further, I let them know, "No, she doesn't have any children."

Now, this may sound a bit pretentious, but the truth is my kids had never seen an apartment before. I had children in my thirties, so by the time they were conscious humans, all our friends were settled into houses. Like anything children experience for the first time, running around her little apartment was excitement number one of the day. After hanging out for a bit, we walked downtown as planned. The kids were fascinated by the simplest things. "Wow, you can get hot dogs right from a cart?" "How can that guy with all those bags of cans balance them while riding a bike?" It was so fun to watch the simplicity (and authenticity) of the brains of my little people that day.

After walking around for a while, we decided to head into Shake Shack to grab some lunch. I asked Nicole if she'd stay with the kids while I grabbed our food at the counter. When I came back to the table, she was doubled over in laughter. I gave her a quizzical look. She looked back with that face that said, *Give me a second, I'll tell you what's up when the kids aren't listening.*

Apparently Mick (four years old at the time) had seized his opportunity to give Nicole some free consulting. Out of the blue he looked at her and said, "You know, if you got a daddy and a baby, you could get a bigger house." Thank God she and I are good friends, and I could laugh at this instead of being completely mortified.

While Mick's strategic advice was a bit embarrassing, he understood that sometimes you have to invest in something in order to get that bigger thing. Mick understood the value (in his mind anyway) of "investing" in a daddy and a baby, so that in turn Nicole could reap the rewards of a bigger house.

Yes, he had veered a bit off course. We all know that investing in a baby daddy isn't necessarily the perfect avenue to home ownership. But he was certainly onto something.

You have to invest if you want to progress.

Where do you land on the age-old debate – what came first, the chicken or the egg?

Although this mind-bending question is older than dirt, we are faced with a similar dilemma all the time. What comes first? Investment or success?

I tuned into this Sucky Song for many years. *Oh yeah, that CTO, of course she's in the big job. Do you know how many nannies she has?* (I never knew the answer, I always just assumed one billion.) Or another favorite of mine: *Of course he's a bigwig. I'm sure his wife stays at home.*

Was I always wrong? Eh, not always. It's true that some successful people do have a shit ton of people helping them out.

But, here are two truths and a lie:

1. People who have big jobs invest first so they can manage taking the big jobs.
2. People who take the big jobs must compromise much of their personal life to take them.

3. The sky is blue.
   (#1 and #3 are the truths in case you weren't sure.)

I know you've used this crutch, my friend. Don't even try and deny it. I've heard you say it before. You have to stop thinking that only the privileged rise. You can stop with the "woe is me" because I'm here to drop this fact on you – most people who find big success have strategically invested in themselves *before* they get the big job.

Successful people don't earn more, then invest. They invest so they can earn more.

I'll never forget the day my husband got his big break. After nine months of grueling interviews, background checks, and polygraphs. After he got kicked out of the process for not attaching his college transcripts and then received a phone call telling him he was back in the process. After years and years of breaking into and then working his way through his new profession, he was hired by a federal three-letter agency.

This was his ultimate job. A career dream.

But.

He would now be forced to commute an hour each way to work. The flexibility he once had in his previous job would be slashed significantly. And that left me thinking, *I might need to quit my job or take another one that is less … everything.*

Our children were four and two years old, both still in daycare, and it was clear to me that we couldn't manage my budding career – especially with all its travel requirements – and have him pursue his dream job at the same time.

And then I realized – there's more than one solution to any problem.

While we had never considered ourselves "nanny people," I thought we might be able to find someone to help us out part time. Someone who could get the kids to daycare when I traveled.

I always tell people that if I had to pick just one thing that helped me say yes to a big career, it was care.com.

Too often we talk about all the nebulous, fluffy stuff. We sit in "rah-rah" conferences and talk about how to be more confident. We coach young women on the power of networking. We tell people if you just speak up, lean in, step up … you'll be all set.

But we don't talk enough about the practical, real-life strategies that make "going for it" possible. For me, that was care.com, a childcare matchmaking site that allowed me to find support. (We've had four part-time nannies over the years, and all have been amazing.) Adding this support was an investment for us. Our household bottom line took an immediate hit. But we invested first, so I could say yes later. We returned that investment hundreds of times over because one of the barriers was lifted. Since that time, my income has nearly tripled. I was able to rise without compromise. All because I realized I needed to invest first.

You're probably rolling your eyes right now. I know what you're thinking. *Yeah, but didn't you feel like you gave up your Mom title to someone else?* Heck no. I never wanted to cross that line. And I didn't. The support we brought on was a fifth arm to help us get through those Oh-fuck-how-the-hell-do-we-manage-this-all? moments. In fact, one of our nannies not only took incredible care of our children but she also became a friend and business partner of mine! If you look at these opportunities less about the transaction and loss of money, and more about the opportunity to grow, magical things can happen.

Remember that time when you had a killer idea at work? The new widget you were going to manufacture that would sell like hotcakes? You pitched it to your boss, and she loved it as much as you did. "Great idea," she said, "but we don't have the money and resources to fund its development."

WTF, right?! So frustrating.

You probably thought something like this: *How the hell does this company expect to ever outpace our competition? Are they idiots?! If we just keep cutting costs, we'll spiral into nothing.*

Your career is your business. If you don't invest first in your career, you're making the same mistake. In fact, much like a business does, you need to set your intention for the future. For example, most companies have a business plan for the following year, which includes the projects they intend to engage in and the money they expect to invest to get there. Think about how your career could benefit from a one-year business plan and some investment. It has the same effect! In fact, you should generally operate with this philosophy:

Spend your money as if you're one year ahead in your journey.

If you went to college, you probably barely blinked an eye before making that ginormous investment. (Well, you might have had other "investors" but still.) The notion of investing first is a no-brainer when it comes to higher education. We then get knee-deep in our careers and we forget to apply the same principle.

Here's how I brought this into my life: Every year when I received my standard raise, I would reinvest a portion of it in some sort of support or growth – housecleaning, coaching, food delivery – anything that either took a piece of the burden off me and my husband or helped us both grow, so we could ultimately give more to our work, our kids, and each other.

What is the biggest thing holding you back from pushing your career further?

If you could add or remove one thing tomorrow, what would it be? Find someone to help you do it. Treat your life and career like it's a business. Invest in its growth.

Spend your money
as if you're
one year ahead
in your journey.

15

Sucky Song #4: I'm already working too hard; the next level will have me working even harder

"Working harder often means you're leading worser."

~ Erin Hatzikostas - author and clearly not an English major

We met for lunch the other day, you and I. Remember our discussion? No? Okay, I'll remind you.

You told me about the long hours you've been working. The 56-slide PowerPoint you've been putting together for your boss' big meeting. The fact that it's the third weekend in a row that you've had to forego a morning workout, and work instead.

And then you said, "I need something new. But I'm good with a lateral move. I can't possibly work more than I already am."

You said you've been in this pattern for years. It feels like the biggest coincidence or maybe the biggest clusterfuck of all time. "Why is this world so crazy?" you asked the air. How could your company expect people to work like they're on a nonstop treadmill, where every month someone comes by and slyly pushes the Up button? You told me you're giving everything you have. And then when you think you can't give any more. Well, you give more.

"But enough is enough," you said. You told me how glad you are that at least you recognize there's more to life. You're determined to stay on this side of the seesaw. And you're okay with rising and rising. You're okay with your feet off the ground a bit. But you're resolved not to let that seesaw launch you into the air. You told me at our "lunch" that you had become convinced there is a direct connection between rising in your career and taking on more work. But that's not true. And if there's one thing you better damn well walk away with after reading this book, it's this: You don't have to take on more work to grow your career.

Sure, there are people who ride the career-life seesaw. But I'm here to tell you, they're doing it wrong.

Here's the truth my friend: People in bigger jobs, who are doing it right, do not work more. In fact, hard work is often due to lazy leadership.

This Sucky Song is likely the one that plays on more Sucky Stations than any other. It's like that Justin Bieber tune that seems to be playing every time you turn on the radio. What this song keeps singing to you is that in each promotion you seek or take, you'll need to work harder because you'll get paid more, have more responsibilities, lead more people, and so on. You think that every step up the rungs of the proverbial ladder will demand more of you. More time, more sacrifice, more everything.

But the truth is, each new promotion and each successive ladder rung isn't asking you to work more. It's asking you to *lead* more. When you take on a job with greater responsibilities, the goal is to achieve greater results, not to work harder. Your focus must continue to shift from grinding it out to leading others. And let me be clear: This does not mean delegation. This means that your focus is on how to better lead a group of people and work in a more elevated way (this even goes for non-manager positions!).

I wrote *You Do You(ish)* while sheltering-in-place during the COVID-19 pandemic. This chapter was just humming along until … school time. You see, my writing happened in our combined office/homework room. My son would start his work just as my creative juices were flowing and my writing came to a crushing halt with, "Mommy, I can't figure this out." "Mommy, is it okay if I do this first?" "Mooommyyyy, I don't get this!"

Do you know what I did? I did exactly what I'm telling you NOT to do. I tried to work harder. Push through it all. Rush through and give answers to his questions and get back to writing as quickly as I could. And then I realized my own truth: You don't go faster by working harder.

When Mick asked if he could show me a video, I reluctantly said yes as my eyes checked the desktop clock. I had so much work to do. He hit play and on came "There's a Hole in My Bucket" (possibly one of the most annoying songs on the planet). I listened and watched as the words flew on the screen and off. But as I continued watching, I realized that this song is a perfect metaphor for this Sucky Song. (Hmm … a metaphor on top of a metaphor. I mentioned I was a math, not English, major, right?)

If you don't recall the lesson from "There's a Hole in My Bucket," I'm not surprised. In summary, this guy has a bucket with a hole in it. He asks the woman (of course) how to fix it. She tells him to use a straw. He tells her it's too long. She tells him to cut it. He asks with what. She tells him a knife. He tells her it's not sharp enough. She tells him to sharpen it with a rock. He says the rock is too dry. She tells him to use water. He asks how to get the water. She tells him, a bucket.

If even that summary of a much longer and more annoying song agitated you, know that it's the same cycle of work craziness you have yourself in. Your bucket is never going to be filled by simply working harder – sawing more straws to try and fill in the bottom of your holey bucket. You must find another approach. And just because you see others patch holes in their buckets to rise in their career, it doesn't mean that's the best way for you.

I used to be you.

As I mentioned, the first role that really stretched me was working in the international arm for Aetna. At the time, Aetna had about fifty thousand employees. It was like working in a small city, with seemingly endless possibilities for new roles and a diverse career in just one place. I was a few months into the new role of leading strategy and business development and expanding our international healthcare presence, when as luck would have it, England released a gigantic Request for Proposal (RFP) to have external companies provide support to their National Healthcare Service. This was a perfect entree and fit for our strategic plan of leveraging our US-centric capabilities and applying them to non-US companies and healthcare systems. My boss took the first leadership step by corralling some volunteers from other parts of the company to help work on our response. This RFP was a beast, and we needed an army to do the months of work on the submission document.

But … (Yep, here it is.) Leading that army sounded daunting. I had spent the last few months entrenched in the strategy and details. I thought, *These helping hands couldn't possibly "get it" as well as I do.* Does this sound familiar? So, I did what many non-leadery people do: I decided to just do most of it myself.

Can you imagine the insane amount of work it took? I knew that I was a smart cookie (why else would they have promoted me in the first place?) and had always been someone who wasn't afraid of hard work. I thought about the time and energy it would take to get these "helpers" up to speed, and instead fell for the same self-talking "crack" I had been addicted to for years – *I'll just do it all myself.*

I didn't get it yet.

I hadn't tasted the alternative addiction: great leadership. I was too caught up in the instant gratification of doing everything myself. I was a bit conceited too (if I'm honest).

Guess what happened? We had mediocre results. It wasn't a complete failure, but we didn't get approved for quite as many business lines as we could have if I'd focused more on leading and less on doing. And the problem with mediocre results is that many times it's just enough to convince ourselves to stay on that do-it-myself crack. Just enough to prevent us from realizing that an addiction to great leadership is much better. If we slow our roll just a little and take the time to invest in others, we'd learn that others aren't as subpar as we think. Investing in others means that our long-term success will not only be greater, it will be SO MUCH EASIER!

I wish I could say that I learned my lesson during my time in that role. I didn't. I was just starting to understand how much

I was running on a one-way treadmill to hell. My real leadership epiphany wouldn't come until many years later, when I got a taste of leadership crack. (And no, I never did actual crack in my life. I just love a smack-you-upside-the-head metaphor.)

I don't want you to fall into the same addiction I fell into — the do-it-all-yourself addiction.

Are you going to have bad days or weeks? Certainly.

We all put in some massive sweat equity from time to time. But I've been hearing this Mayday call for years. Maybe not from you. But from a lot of people who aren't much different than you. I'm sure you've had your moments. And I implore you to slow the frick down and ask yourself, *Am I addicted to doing things myself? What one small change can I make to start leading others to help me get stuff done?*

I want you to think about implementing a new "law" to change your addiction and rewrite this Sucky Song.

Leadership Law: Sacrifice short-term *productivity* for long-term *positivity*.

It is difficult hard to slow down and bring others along. I get it. But when you break your addiction to doing and instead focus on getting addicted to leading, that's when amazing things happen. When you start to focus less on checking the box and more on meeting with people, developing them, teaching them, that's what will allow you to achieve the success you crave and deserve. Sometimes it takes a while, but just as often it doesn't. People are smarter than you think. Slow down your freight train and let them aboard.

And there's also a chorus to this "I'm already working too hard" Sucky Song, which is part of the problem. The chorus goes something like this: "But I don't have anyone who works for me. How can I possibly get help and lead others?"

I want you to turn off that song and never turn it on again. Do you hear me?!

The best leaders do not wait to have authority. The best leaders lead without authority. In fact, I promoted many people into management positions after I saw them lead without anyone reporting to them. Experimenting and practicing great leadership is best done with people you don't sign the paycheck for. For people who don't follow simply because they feel like they have to.

Finally, let me fess up on something.

I'm still you … sometimes. This, like everything I preach in this book, is one big practice playground. I still have days where I'm running around like the Cathy cartoon. Hair flailing, heart pumping, not leading, and instead doing all the schtuff myself. And I've also progressed. Significantly. All because I kept practicing and keeping my hand on the radio dial. Keep making small steps to turn the dial to a Suck-cess Song, like "One Thing Leads to Another" by The Fixx. If you do, you'll work less and inspire more. You'll be able to say yes to more. Without working more. Maybe even less. Trust me.

16

Sucky Song #5: I'm not good at office politics, so I can't play with the big boys and girls

"Be who you are and say what you feel,
because those that mind don't matter,
and those that matter don't mind."

~ Bernard M. Baruch - economist,
philanthropist and Dr. Suess inspirer

Oh yes, this swan song. The album cover says "I'm not good at office politics, so I'm not going to even think about moving up to the next level." In fact, I just heard this one again yesterday at a small socially distanced gathering at our house. (Ahh … we'll remember these days forever, won't we?) Some great friends of ours were over. One is the CIO of a major company. His wife is a total badass IT program manager who decided to take a break (which I applaud). We were discussing this book when she started to talk about how, although she was a kickass leader, she just didn't have the "politics" in her. Even her husband piped in and confirmed that she just wouldn't have been able to handle what they both referred to as the AVP level — "Always Very Politicizing."

I cringed. Sighed. And said, "But you know you can always rewrite how things are done, right?"

There will be some crazy personalities to contend with as you climb the ladder. Whether in the traditional corporate setting, in a school, or at a nonprofit. There will always be those people that float to the top. You're not required to play the same game they're playing. In fact, if you can stop thinking about your interactions as *politics* and instead, think of them as *connections*, it can change everything. Office politics are often like a sorority. From the outside, the office seems fake, but once inside, you realize that it's mostly made up of real connections with just a few bad apples.

If there's one thing I'm good at, and I'm going to make sure you're also damn good at, it's creating authentic connections with people. We'll dive into this more deeply in a later chapter, but I want to start laying the groundwork for a new tune here. You've been brainwashed into believing that you have to network and politic, and this falsehood has distracted you from seeing that it's simpler than that. All of life, career included, is about creating connections with people. And yes, some are way easier than others. I challenge you, though, to have fun with those more difficult ones. Some of my fondest memories were when I knew I had to win over a tough person.

I recall a particular meeting with a prospective customer. In the meeting they had one of their consultants attend, and it didn't take me long to spot this grumpy older man. I thought, *I'm going to make sure I sit next to this guy and work him like there's no tomorrow.*

As the meeting got underway, every few comments he made I would be sure to call him out for his intelligent thoughts. I also found an opportune time to crack a joke aimed his way, to see if I could lighten him up. And every five minutes or so, I would slide my chair ever so slightly his way, creating this literal "connection." By the end of the meeting, we were chatting away and laughing.

Victory!

I get it. You might be like, "That's soooo not me." You're likely right. My authentic approach may not be yours. I'm also sure you have your own experiences in winning over people. Maybe it was connecting with a college roommate you were sure you were never going to like. Maybe you even won over your partner after they didn't know you existed. Or I'm sure you've had a colleague or two who started out as a foe, and now you're friends. We all have the ability to rise to challenges like this. It's a matter of understanding just what your best tools are for winning people over.

Stop seeing it as office politics and start seeing it as office partnerships.

Change the tune. Rewrite this Sucky Song.

And look, you cannot eradicate sucky people. But if you focus on finding ways to connect, you'll begin to look at those people less as brick walls and more as challenges to overcome. You may even start to inspire them to be less sucky, as you lead by example. There's so much crappy behavior in the workplace because many people have seen others "above them" behave crappily. Not enough people have the cojones to do things their own way.

That's what I want from you. I want you to not just change your tune for your own good, I want you to change your tune for the tens, hundreds, or even thousands of people who will admire and be inspired by your new way of doing things.

As I mentioned before, authenticity is contagious. So why don't we see more authenticity in the workplace? Why do we see so many unhappy people?

Because not enough people have stepped up and shown them a new path. They're waiting for inspiration from people like you. I want you to jam out to this new Suck-cess Song you've created. Not just for you, but for others. Do it for the next generation of leaders. Do it for your children, who are watching you demonstrate. Do it for the authenticity movement. Do it for you.

Dance when you're not supposed to dance

A few years ago, when I was still the CEO of my previous company, we hosted our first ever leaders' forum. We were gathering our one hundred leaders for an event intended to kick off a company-wide cultural shift. I was responsible for opening and closing the two-day summit. Since this was about inspirational leadership, it was pretty darn important that my messages be, well, inspiring.

In the days leading up to the forum, our consultant sent me a video (which had gone viral) of a guy at a concert who begins dancing and inspires everyone else to join in. Obviously, it was a fun metaphor for leadership and how infectious positive energy and inspiration can be. It was cute, I guess. They wanted me to include it in my closing. I had other ideas.

Just hours before kickoff, the coaches requested a huddle to go over my closing speech. I said to the huddle crew, "I saw the video. I agree it's inspiring, but instead of showing it, I'm just going to dance."

I got deep looks of concern and comments like "Okay … but are you sure you caught the voice over? The really powerful message it offers?"

We started the video again. About twenty seconds in, I shut it down.

Me: "Okay, here's the thing. I understand the message and what it's trying to get across. But this guy isn't really a leader. He's probably drunk. And the people that start dancing, they're probably drunk too."

At this point, the people in the room looked like *they'd* rather be drunk than entertain the idea of me dancing on stage.

I decided to probe. "Let me ask you this: Are you worried that we're going to have an amazing few days and then I'm going to ruin it by dancing? Or are you worried that I'm going to make an ass of myself?"

The answer was unanimous. "We're not worried about that first thing."

"Great, it's settled then. I'm dancing."

When it came time to close, I stood on stage and went through my prepared remarks. Then we put up just one slide, which said, "The first follower is what transforms a lone nut into a leader" — a quote by Derek Sivers in one of his TED Talks.

Cue music.

I started dancing.

I looked nuts.

But only for a few seconds. As I predicted, someone else started dancing almost immediately. Then another. Within fifteen seconds, the entire room of one hundred people was dancing.

After it was over, the team came up to me and attendees said things like "I can't imagine a better way to end such an incredible few days." It was different. It was vulnerable. It was energizing. It was just the kind of unexpected leadership that people were craving.

Dance where you're not supposed to dance. Especially when people tell you not to. Your soul is meant to dance.

PART 3

Who Says Authenticity Can't Be Your Secret Weapon?

17

We are human after all

"The main thing in life is not to be afraid of being human."

~ Aaron Carter - singer, dancer, and producer

Now that we've tuned out the Sucky Songs and into Suck-cess Songs, you're ready. In this next section, we're going to dive deep into the Six Principles of Strategic Authenticity, featuring the acronym, HUMANS. I'll be teaching you how to unlock and unleash your authentic self and use it as your secret weapon for success.

I want you to think of this like running. Yes, I know there's a good chance you hate running. But what we're doing here together is similar to training for a run.

I've been running the authenticity race for many years. I'm a few marathons in. You might need to do an authenticity walk/jog for a while at first, and then I'll help you jog your way up to an authenticity 5K. Yet if you're one of the bolder ones, you might sprint right past me, fueled by permission and the confidence that you can use your authentic badassness to cruuuush it. My hope is to make this the most enjoyable, easy, and self-serving "training" you've done in a long time.

No matter where you are on the authenticity running spectrum, what you learn here is going to help you fall more and more in love with the authenticity journey … the run. I hope you're a little nervous but also able to revel in the glory of the hard pushes. At some point, you'll start looking at the scenery when you're out for some authenticity training. And I want you to inspire others to run their own authenticity races too.

Now, remember when I said that authenticity does not simply mean "be yourself," that it's actually more complicated than that? Over the past few years, I've spent a lot of time researching, reflecting, and reading about authenticity so that I could put a structure — a sort of map — to something that, until now, most people believed was elusive. I began by considering how I'd brought authenticity into my work-life toolkit.

My success wasn't simply *me being me* and letting that fly into the world. I doubled down on being authentic. I felt a calling to more deeply understand it and put together a framework that anyone could use for their own authentic success. I wanted to define it in a way that would carefully balance the fact that authenticity is inherently personal with the fact that I also believe it's more nuanced and formulaic than most people think.

The Six Principles of Strategic Authenticity are the essential ingredients in my personal authenticity recipe and are the features we observe in those around us that makes us say, "Ah-ha, that person is so authentic." While my focus is on the use of authenticity in the workplace, these principles have incredible power in your personal life as well.

I mentioned above that these principles conveniently (okay, with a little finagling) fall into the acronym HUMANS. We're going to walk through each of these in a way that I hope will inspire, encourage, and give you practical to-dos to use authenticity as your new secret weapon.

So, get on your best sweat suit and let's hit the road.

Six Principles of Strategic Authenticity

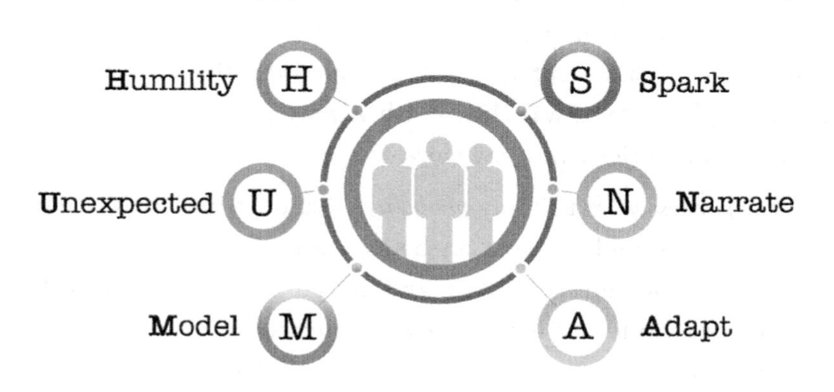

18

Humility: Cooking up some humble pie

"If I only had a little humility,
I'd be perfect."

~ Ted Turner - authentic and outspoken business guy, CNN founder, and philanthropist

Let's start with an A/B test. Pretend we just met, and I'm still in my corporate role. We're at a business meeting, going through the standard introductions and "background checks" that kick off most big meetings. When it's my turn, I can choose one of two paths.

PATH A:

Hi, my name is Erin Hatzikostas and I've spent over twenty years in the healthcare industry in various leadership positions. I've held roles in actuarial, underwriting, product development, and provider network management. In 2012, I joined PayFlex and led Strategy and Business Development, then I took over Marketing and eventually became the COO. Now I'm CEO. Nice to meet you.

PATH B:

When I was a sophomore in college, my roommate announced that being an actuary was the perfect career for me because I was so good at math. After convincing Aetna to hire me into their actuarial program, I quickly realized that being an actuary was a major mismatch with my Myers-Briggs profile. Not to mention, I couldn't pass an exam to save my life. I decided to pivot and was afforded many incredible opportunities at the company, including leading Aetna's international healthcare expansion, our national accounts provider network team, and most recently, I joined PayFlex. I initially joined just to lead Business Development. And well, every time someone left the company, they kept giving more things to me, until I eventually became the CEO. Nice to meet you.

Which one of these introductions is more intriguing?

I hope you said Path B. Don't you just find yourself zoning out when people give a typical, boring, and boastful introduction? I've been giving some version of the Path B introduction for years.

Why?

The power of humility.

There are a few things we can glean from the Path B introduction. But let's first focus on the components of humility.

HUMILITY MUST BE SINCERE

Sure, I was being a bit flippant when I told the story above. Yet I was also sincere. I admitted my imperfections. I did fail at my actuarial career. The actuarial field requires you to take a series of exams, none of which I passed, so by any measure I can sincerely claim failure here. (Not that a binary pass/fail is a requirement of humility.) Also, my promotions in PayFlex all came on the heels of someone leaving … but don't most?

• • • • • • •

Humility is not a
fishing
(for a compliment)
expedition.

• • • • • • • •

We all know someone who puts themselves down so they can be rewarded by another person telling them they're wrong and paying them a compliment. As C.S. Lewis said, "Humility is not thinking less of yourself, but thinking of yourself less." Humility is showing that you're able to admit to and sometimes even shine a spotlight on those things that make you an imperfect human.

Being humble makes you more mindful, keeps you open to continuous learning, and makes you a more inviting person to be around. But I want to teach you how to *use* humility for your own benefit.

THE HUMILITY HALO

I have a strong belief that humility is a dynamic tool to create connections with others. I was looking forward to writing about this in *You Do You(ish)*, and I figured I would find great third-party scientific evidence to support my hypothesis. Except I didn't.

What I found was that the current research on humility is quite vague and incomplete. While there were articles on humble leadership that discuss how humility creates trust within a team, I didn't find substantive studies that drew a straight line from humility to impact.

Humility is powerful.

Integrating humility into the way you interact with others creates a sort of "halo effect" – a Humility Halo. The halo effect that comes when you're humble is almost like a "pay it forward" – later judgments are more likely to be positive because folks have seen you're willing to expose your faults. It's like having money in the bank towards a later debt.

When used as a tool, humility does three critical things:

1. creates connections with people more quickly
2. increases trust
3. creates intrigue

CONNECTION

Humility is like a Disney FastPass to connection.

Reflect for a moment on how connected you felt to me when I introduced myself using Path A. On a scale of 1 to 10, compare that to your feelings about me when I spoke the Path B script. You see, when we add in a dose of humility, people immediately think, *They're like me: imperfect.* You open up a small window to the part of your soul that's messy and sticky and gooey. People have a much easier time connecting to something with a little bit of messy goo.

Humility whizzes you past the long line of the "waiting to

get to know you." It bypasses all the bullshit. Humble language implies that you aren't going to pretend to be perfect and you're inviting the other person to reveal their imperfections too. The other person can imagine having a beer with you and shootin' the shit. The faster you can get to that level of connectedness, the more you can get done together.

TRUST

At work, we continuously have our trust-o-meter running. We gauge trust with new people we meet and with those we've known for years. Trust is always being evaluated. You might not be conscious of it, but this trust-o-meter is running in your head (and everybody else's) nonstop, assessing if the amount you trust someone is increasing, decreasing, or remaining the same.

And the number one question that drives that meter is, Are they hiding anything? The first step to determining if you can trust someone is knowing if you can expect them to be forthright with you.

It's likely you've come to expect difficult things at work, like disagreements, mistakes, and receiving negative feedback. You know that shit hits the fan from time to time. And you want to trust that the people you interact with will do their best to give you the truth. At. All. Times.

So how does that translate here? If you embrace your flaws and expose them, it's a game changer. When people see you wearing your flaws out in the open, they tend to put down the trust-o-meter and relax. And once people have trust in you, it's more likely to be reciprocated. They'll do what they can to win that same level of trust from you.

We shouldn't *distrust* our flaws but instead use our flaws to *create* trust.

INTRIGUE

This is the least obvious trait of the Humility Halo, yet it's the most fun. I like to think that strategically using humility is akin to when singers use a low, soft tone at the beginning of a song. The best singers don't start with the big note, the peppy tempo, or maximum volume. They start low and slow, showing off a range of notes and increasing volume in the lead up to a big crescendo. Consciously adding humility creates similar variation, which takes your colleagues on a journey with you. Leveraging humility is most powerful when you treat it like a song. You unveil your humility in small doses here and there in encounters with people. Then, after you've done that for a while, your big crescendo (a "big brag" moment) hits your audience in a much more powerful way.

For example, I use humility in my introductions to people when I talk about my actuarial failure. This is my low and slow melody line. Then later, when I want to talk about how much I crushed it as a CEO or mention the massive results we had, it's better received. My "big brag" crescendo is perceived as less arrogant because I've laid out all the ways that I'm not perfect.

Essentially, using humility lets you highlight what a badass you are, without looking cocky. Humility also helps you build some mystery or intrigue into who you are so that people will be interested in learning more about you or want to be around you more so they can see what else you'll reveal. They become curious about you. What will she say? What will he do? You can be both the person who walks in the room making fun of yourself *and* the one that comes in strutting your stuff.

When you're willing to expose a fault, people can't help but wonder what else is in your vault.

So how do you want to begin cooking up some humble pie?

Some of you might be able to take a few of my stories, put down the book, and start running. But for others this might feel less natural. Sure, you're not a boastful person ... some may even call you humble. But how do you actually *use* humility to strengthen your career? Well, my friend, I have a few tools for you.

HUMILITY MOMENTS

A few months ago, I was in a two-day mastermind session, learning more about how to craft a great keynote speech. Guess what the very first element was: self-deprecating humor. (Which essentially is humility with a side of something to make people laugh.) When listening to professional speakers, you'll notice that intentional humility is at the forefront of their talks, for all the reasons I explained above: connection, trust, and intrigue.

As part of my speech-writing process, I have a list of humility traits, stories, and moments at the ready. They're not just in my head but written into a document on my computer. Anytime I'm preparing a new talk, I go to this list for inspiration, and I include at least one of them.

I want you to start by making a similar list – we'll call this your Humility Moments List. These things will be your building blocks. When the time comes, you can draw from these to start creating your own Humility Halo. Grab a pen and paper or go to your computer and write down the answers to some or all of these questions:

Humility Moments List

- What's a subject you suck at?
- What physical feature are you self-conscious of?
- What bad habit do you have?
- What's the biggest work project you've ever screwed up?
- What's something you've failed miserably at?
- What do you hate doing?
- What's a recent mini-disaster you just went through? (Hint: Stories about working from home with kids are ripe for the picking.)
- What other stories do you have that highlight a moment where you messed up?

Next, think about places you can sprinkle in these Humility Moments. Team meetings, interviews, presentations, and so forth. This isn't a onetime thing. Start small and use some humility in a meeting with people you already know. Experiment. Just try it and see what happens. Practice, practice, practice.

CYCLE OF HUMILITY

Learning to use humility as an ingredient to your success occurs in a cycle.

As with anything I inspire in this book, adding humility is not a one-and-done. I don't want you to wake up tomorrow and think, *Time to put that new humble me into strategic action.*

Instead, start with small experiments. Begin by becoming more self-aware.

What's one simple (and maybe a bit funny) flaw that you have? Get comfortable with it, embrace it. See it as an important part of what makes you you. Then think about how you can expose it. Where might you be able to talk about this flaw? It doesn't have to be in a group setting. It's just as effective when you're working with someone mano a mano. Ask yourself: *How can I open up a conversation with a team member?* How can I use that to connect more deeply with them? How can I use it to demonstrate a point I've been trying to make for years?

For example, "Lisa, I know your team just messed up that report. But it's okay to make mistakes. Let me tell you about a time when I shit the bed on a big project. And here's what happened as a result …"

I bet I know what you're thinking right about now. In fact, you may have been thinking about this on and off for much of the book. *But Erin, what if I [work for an asshole] or [am surrounded by assholes] or [have colleagues that are narcissists]?* Know this: The things I teach you about authenticity as a strategy at work are even better when you're dealing with assholes.

Because, my friend, you're not simply "being yourself," you're leveraging authenticity as a strategy. And you can dial this up and down however it serves you. You also can't beat assholes at their own game. You need *your* own game. Your own strategy. Authenticity is the water to their fire.

Try one new thing, starting at the top of the Circle of Humility; use some flaw and take it on a test drive. Be mindful of what you feel when you do this and really tune in to people's reactions.

Turn your superflaws into your superpowers.

Ultimately, I want you to see your flaws as your gifts. Used in the right way, your relationships will grow and strengthen when you use the power of humility. As I mentioned before, this can't be insincere – you have to wear your shortcomings on your sleeve. Just as importantly though, you must match your humble moments with big brag moments.

Creating a Humility Halo isn't about being an angel. It's about being self-aware, vulnerable, and courageous. It's about seeking the fastest way to connect and gain trust. It's about creating a little mystery in who you are and ultimately having people follow you, if only out of curiosity.

Wait, you're not Aaron?

We wrapped up a full day of our women-let's-do-this! conference. You know the kind. A bunch of women work their asses off to plan and execute their own women's conference. If I'm brutally honest, I think they're kinda bullshit. In many of them we spend way too much time talking about the problems and not enough time talking about the solutions. Not to mention, the format is often stuffy, the food barely gets touched, and there's never enough laughter. Or wine.

I admit though, I used to be part of these. Now I'm focused (alongside my podcast co-host) on reinventing women's conferences. If you ever come to one of ours, hold on to your hat. Think less pontificating and more dancing. Less lecture and more conjecture. Less confining and much more wining.

But a few years back, I was the co-chair of our enterprise's women's group, specifically focused on advancing women into the executive ranks. We held a one-day conference. Gina Davis spoke and was amazing. The rest was ... well ... typical.

The *very* next day (hold on to this detail, the irony is off the charts), I drove up to Massachusetts for a town hall meeting that my boss' boss was hosting. I had been asked to do a round-robin section, which essentially meant that I had no more than two minutes to talk about something.

When I got to the office, I went to check in with the in-house TV guys (yes, we had our own studio) to see what the drill was for the meeting. It's important to note that these are guys I had worked with on several occasions. They knew who I was.

Note: The names I use here are not their real names so as to keep it confidential (and save others from potential embarrassment.)

I popped into the makeshift audiovisual room and asked Dude, "What's the plan? Anything I should be aware of before we go live?"

Dude looked at me and said, "You're not talking today."

Like two siblings arguing, we went on …

"Yes, I am."

"No, you're not."

I asked Dude to pull up the PowerPoint for evidence. I said, "Scroll down. See, I'm doing the round-robin."

Dude looked at me and said, "No, you're not. This morning I talked to Guy and he said that Aaron and Buddy were doing that section."

I looked at him and said, "*I am Erin*. You know that, Dude."

"Oooooh, I assumed he meant *male* Aaron."

Sometimes you get lucky enough to have ridiculously great stories just land in your lap.

19

Unexpected: The love punch they didn't see coming

"Different is better than better."

~ Sally Hogshead - NYT best-selling author, NSA Hall of Fame speaker, CEO of How to Fascinate, and someone I totally agree with

When I developed the Six Principles of Strategic Authenticity, I spent a lot of time debating whether the "U" in HUMANS should be "unexpected" or "unique." I felt this was an important decision and distinction. I concluded that it's being *unexpected* that *uniquely* makes authenticity such a powerful strategy.

There are examples of this in action everywhere. Jacinda Ardern, prime minister of New Zealand, is one that I have been obsessed with recently. If you're like me, you had no idea who she was until the COVID-19 pandemic hit in 2020. Her response to the crisis shot her onto the global podium of recognition and admiration. If you drill down on what made her so effective, you'll find it was neither her innovation nor her uniqueness. It was that she did things that were unexpected. Take for example how she handled communicating to the citizens of her country early in the crisis. While using social media isn't a new technique for national leaders, she used it in an unexpected way. Rather than letting social media simply be a megaphone, projecting her message one way to the populace, she showed up on Facebook Live in order to listen as well. And in a beautiful twist of unexpectedness, she did so in a worn-out hoodie while admitting that she had just put her young daughter to bed.

This is an example of how being even slightly unexpected can create power. As Jacinda showed, if you combine a little unexpected (Facebook Live) with a sprinkle of humility (old sweatshirt), you are able to influence people with authenticity in a powerful way. In this case, she saved lives. As of mid-December 2020, New Zealand recorded only twenty-five deaths from COVID. Twenty-five! Sure, they are an island nation that has fewer than five million people, but those results taken per capita are still some of the best in the world. Her unexpected, authentic approach gained the trust of her citizens and created incredible results.

Here's the good news: You don't have to be a world leader or a genius to be unexpected. You don't have to invent some new personality trait or be cutting edge. You simply have to continually wonder, *What do people expect, and how can I give them something that's a bit different?*

Here's one for you. When you jump on a Zoom call a few minutes late, instead of saying something like "I'm sorry I was a few minutes late" (what everyone says), say something that is true but unexpected, such as "Sorry I'm late. My son just flushed his sister's favorite doll down the toilet, and I was scrambling to try and save it!"

THE SCIENCE OF UNEXPECTED

There is fascinating research into the unforeseen. In the book *Surprise: Embrace the Unpredictable and Engineer the Unexpected* by Tania Luna, the author dives deep into the power behind being unexpected (i.e., surprises). When you're exposed to something unexpected, it triggers a "surprise sequence" in your brain. The cognitive resources in our brains (the ones that build, create, and solve) are hijacked and taught to stand at attention and get curious about what else might go down.

Have you ever been frustrated that someone you're working with might not be giving you their full attention? I know what you're thinking ... *Like every frickin' moment of the day, Erin.* Think of being unexpected as a way to scream out like a teacher in an elementary school class, "One, two, three. All eyes on me!"

The brain of your colleague goes through a sequence after you've enacted some moment of unexpectedness:

- They stop other thoughts and tasks.
- They become curious.
- They want to know what's coming next.
- They reach over to their flight dashboard and unclick the autopilot button, put on their glasses, and lean forward to get a clearer view of what may be on the horizon.

After that, they start to change how they were thinking about something. This is important because, without an interrupting stimulus like this, people's brains keep going down the same old tracks. The Taser blast you just gave them will open their mind to other possibilities, like the limited way they've been thinking about a project. Or it could be as simple as how they've been thinking about you.

A basic example of this is the way I started a meeting just the other day. It was a 4:00 meeting with a potential business partner. At 4:33 that same day, the first SpaceX shuttle was planned to launch. I was looking forward to the meeting, but I was also thinking, *We gotta wrap this thing up early because we can't be talking business blah-de-blah-blah while the first-ever Elon Musk space shuttle is taking off.* So, when the CEO of the company hopped onto the call a few minutes late, I said, "Were you just Googling everything under the sun about this space launch to answer your kids' questions? 'Cause that's what I was doing." And yes, that truly was what I was doing in the minutes leading up the call because I didn't know how NASA was working with SpaceX ... or when the last shuttle launch was ... or how often people go to space on average ... or if NASA was still government funded.

So, I threw out a little authentic and unexpected intro. I stirred up a little bit of curiosity about who I am. I signaled that this meeting wasn't going to be your ordinary zzzzz. And I also signaled, *I will probably run out of this Zoom call at 4:32, so let's get this show on the road!*

Authenticity is about exposing who you are, when people least expect it.

Authenticity, in some part, is derived from not knowing what's coming next. Making people realize they can't predict what they're going to hear from you proves to them that you're not a walking, talking PowerPoint deck. NOBODY likes to be in a meeting where the bullets of info are put up a few minutes before the presenter reads them verbatim. It's boring and it's maddening!

Now think about someone who made it obvious that they weren't going be predictable. Think of someone who always has their hand resting precariously on the crank of a jack-in-the-box. At any point, it might pop up. That's a hell of a lot more fun, right? It also rewires your brain to wake the fuck up, stop anticipating only the typical, and start thinking outside the (jack-in-the-) box!

Lemme guess what you're thinking right now … *Please give me some training wheels so I don't immediately fall flat on my face.*

I got you. Here are some ideas:

Unexpected Starter Kit

- In a serious meeting, insert a light joke.
- In a lighter meeting, get serious about a topic just after the group finishes laughing at something.
- Instead of starting a meeting with an agenda, start it with a story (more on that later).
- Insert a funny or personal picture into a traditional presentation.
- Join a video conference in your sweaty athletic gear.
- Use a quote from your favorite comedy to demonstrate a serious point.

- Send someone a thank-you card when they least expect it.
- Wear sneakers to a keynote presentation (check out the ones I wore in my TEDx Talk, "Why you don't have to compromise for your career").

If this waking people up and getting them to pay more attention to you wasn't enough to get you to buy into the power of being unexpected, I want to throw a few other "sur-prizes" at you. These just add to the business case of always being sure you're giving people something they didn't see coming.

UNEXPECTED SUR-PRIZE #1

The first is humor. After all, being unexpected is a top technique of comedians, speakers, and writers. One of the best ways to make people laugh is to say something they aren't expecting.

While I didn't make "humor" a core ingredient of the Six Principles of Strategic Authenticity, consider it the spice you add to your authenticity dinner. Just like every meal could use a pinch of salt and pepper, every interaction is strengthened by some humor.

You likely think of yourself as at least a little bit funny, right? Perfect. You don't have to be a professional comedian in order to be funny. And humor needn't be contrived. Subtle and small attempts at humor can stir things up. Bring the unexpected to work with you and you'll organically become a funny person. I can't write a joke to save my life, but people think I'm funny. It's mostly because I often say something unexpected.

One of my favorite recent social media memes is a great example (unknown origin).

Therapist [over the phone]: "Do you think the quarantine has changed you?"

Me [knitting a dress for the possum in my backyard]: "No."

Unexpectedness at its finest.

UNEXPECTED SUR-PRIZE #2

Being unexpected is also a weapon in the "underdog battle." Aren't we all an underdog in some way? Your gender, your education, your work experience … we all have some sort of underdog status. Whatever yours is, own it, capitalize on it, and roll it into your unexpected menu.

I have a great story to illustrate this one.

When I was in college, I was a calculus tutor. Apparently, the fact that I was female, in a sorority, and had long blond hair was incongruent with the image folks had of a calculus tutor. When I walked into a session, I'd inevitably be approached by some well-meaning tutor who would ask if I needed help.

I LOVED it. This didn't upset me. I loved that they assumed I was a student in need of help. This love of surprising people has never waned for me. I don't hate walking into a room full of men as the only woman. I don't hate that people think I look too young, too hip, and maybe even a bit too flighty to be a CEO (yes, I've heard that). And I don't hate that people presume my husband has been our breadwinner. Why? Because this is fertile ground to surprise. This is fuel, people! Surprising them is the quickest way to grab their attention, after which you can speed the hell past the BS and get shit done.

Like with every trick in this book, you won't be flipping a switch. Consider using the power of the unexpected as more of a dimmer switch. Dial it up just a bit one time and crank it to retina-burning bright another. The hue you shine at depends on the situation you're in and where you are in your authenticity training. Because my muscles are so used to running this race, I'm constantly on the prowl for opportunities to surprise people. *Normal* should become your kryptonite. Understand that predictable isn't going to get you the full impact you desire. Shine bright on a regular basis. Remember to be curious, experiment, and have courage to nudge things a little more toward uncomfortable, toward the unexpected, each time you walk into a meeting.

Watch what
everyone else
is doing.
And then
do the opposite.

20 Model: Show don't tell

"Be the change that you wish to see in the world."

~ Mahatma Gandhi - the man, the myth, the legend

No, this is not the part of the book where I turn you into Gisele Bündchen. It is, however, where I'm going to essentially ask you to shut up a bit and instead *show up*.

Can you recall the last time you had one of those "Ahh, they're so authentic" moments when you were observing someone? It's highly likely it wasn't caused by what the person *said*. It's more likely that it was how they *acted*.

About three years ago, I got to see (and hug!) one of the most authentic and beautiful humans on the face of this earth: Michelle Obama. I'd had a chick-crush on Michelle for years. I always admired her grace, beauty, and intellect, which are magnificently juxtaposed with her humility, humor, and sass.

I was blessed to have been invited by Karen Lynch, a sponsor of mine and executive at Aetna (who was recently named as the CEO of CVS). Karen had ten tickets to Michelle's event at our local theater, as well as backstage passes to meet her. We had seats just three rows back from the stage. As we sat waiting for the event to begin, I could feel the tension building in the room. Buzzing really. Michelle was standing somewhere behind the curtains, possibly only a few feet from where we sat and waited.

I will never forget the moment she walked on stage. Her smile lit up the entire room. Everything about her ... the setting, her mood, the entire night was completely authentic. The stage had only two chairs and a table where the moderator, Thelma Golden, sat and asked Michelle questions, almost like two girlfriends catching up on one of their living room couches.

The very first question Thelma threw out to Michelle was "Is there anything that you know now that you wish you would have known when you first entered the White House?" Without a second thought, Michelle's response came flying out of her mouth almost in one long run-on sentence. It felt like she was recalling the entire day for the very first time, right alongside all of us. It went something like this:

I remember it was so cold that day we were standing outside for the inauguration, freezing, we then had to go on this really long parade and we were still so cold, then we get to the White House and they are taking us here and there and all of a sudden I was like, "Hold up, where are my kids? Who took my kids?" Then we went straight to one gala after another ... I remember standing on the dance floor and Barack spun me out, held my hand, and I looked at him and thought, Wait, you? You're the president? *It was such a crazy, whirlwind day.*

She paused and looked at Thelma Golden and said, "Oh gosh, wait, what was the question?"

She went on for the next hour telling us story after story. Hilarious recounts of how Malia had resting-bitch-face (RBF) for much of the time Barack was in office. She told a story about a time when they were at an official event, cameras everywhere, and she kept nudging Malia to smile. Then Michelle showed us how Malia looked when she said, "Mom, I *am* smiling!" — all while keeping the same RBF. Michelle talked about growing up on the South Side of Chicago and how to this day she still hangs out with all the same people, just like she did well before she became a prominent lawyer, and her husband became the most powerful man on earth. Throughout the evening, you could hear the room collectively having hundreds of "ah-ha" moments.

Why? Because she was modeling the behavior we all want for ourselves. She didn't give us fancy anecdotes and pithy quotes. She demonstrated a person we all want to be. She gave us permission through her actions more than through her words. All these ah-ha moments occurred because our experience with her wasn't two-dimensional; it felt three-dimensional. She touched every one of our five senses.

Of all the Six Principles of Strategic Authenticity, Model may feel the most intangible. It may also be most impactful to you. I'll bring this concept to life so you can see how it can affect you and others. Plus, I'll talk about how it will help you operate with a fresh perspective that will no longer have you thinking you have to compromise one thing for another.

If you're like most human beings, you primarily operate using a Manage Mindset. That is, you're focused on the direct, tangible actions you need to take to get work done, to raise your kids, to lead others. It's not bad, but it's not sustainable or optimal. A Manage Mindset puts too much emphasis on what you say, what you accomplish in the short term, and what you *should* do and say.

I want you to start shifting to a Model Mindset. Much like how Michelle operated that night and in everything she does, someone with a Model Mindset is less focused on *saying* the right words and more focused on *acting* the right way.

Let me get more work-tactical for you. Let's say you're leading a highly technical project at work, and you know that if the team doesn't predict and prevent every potential issue, there's a high probability that the project launch will be a mess. If you're using a Manage Mindset, you'll do things like …

- Tell the team (multiple times) about the importance of making sure to think of everything.
- Say the words "Be sure to think of everything" (a lot).
- Go through the team's project plans and ask them to ensure they've tested everything.

Here's the problem: People become impervious to words and most likely will not change their behavior. The impact you get from a Manage Mindset is incremental. A Manage Mindset will move you forward but not with the force and exponential growth you and others desire.

Now let's talk about a Model Mindset. If you adopt this mindset, you'll focus on demonstrating what you want from others. In the same project scenario, you'll do things like …

- Lead a meeting where you ask someone to poke holes in assumptions you made on your part of the project.
- Ask the team questions, like "What else?" when they challenge you and your assumptions, demonstrating that you want to go deeper than ever before.

- Hold a separate meeting with the development team to talk through your requirements, then bring that back to the broader team as an example of a way to operate that ensures they leave no stone unturned.

The impact you get from a Model Mindset is exponential. People are more likely to change and improve when they see someone else doing the same.

People listen to words but they emulate action.

This isn't rocket science. This is how we learn. Children don't learn to walk by being told how to do it, they learn by watching bigger humans walk. This doesn't end when we become adults. But unfortunately, we get so darned sophisticated with our words and our business buzzword bingo that we get further and further from this principle, which was the foundation for how we learned for much of our earlier lives.

Manage Mindset	Model Mindset
Say the right words	Demonstrate the right behavior
How much time I spend	How much inspiration I create
Short-term impact	Long-term impact
Operate in 2-D	Operate in 3-D
Self-less (care more about others than yourself)	Self-plus (care more about what the collective can do: you + others)

It's not your fault if you're operating largely with a Manage Mindset. This mindset slowly takes over as you get more entrenched in a world that rewards tangible actions. You slip into a pattern of managing people, situations, kids — managing through it all. Instead, adopting (or getting back to) a Model Mindset allows you to shift your focus away from talking and doing, and bring it back to putting much of your energy into modeling the outcome/behavior/feeling you want others to have.

I use my Model Mindset to preach authenticity. Yes, I have to say and write words. But my Model Mindset is always forcing me to ask myself, *But am I demonstrating authenticity?* This might sound simple, but it's easy to slip away from a Model Mindset. It's easy to get caught up in the how-tos and shoulds of the world. For example, I'm in a new profession, and continuously learning things like how to write an email that will engage people, how to craft a great keynote, or how to write a book. When learning new things, it's easy to get caught up in what you should do and forget that people will be most affected by what you model for them not by what you tell them. My Model Mindset is always being challenged, but as I continue to embrace it as my modus operandi, modeling goes more and more on autopilot.

A Model Mindset doesn't just result in exponential impact at work. Adopting a Model Mindset is a crucial shift, especially for working parents. It allows you to realize that it's not the everyday, go-through-the-motions stuff you do for your children that matters the most. It's the big example that you set for them in how you work, live, and love.

As I mentioned in Sucky Song #1, reframing your role as a parent to one that is focused on demonstrating versus suffocating is key to understanding it's okay to have the career you want. It's not selfish. It's actually self-PLUS. You realize that your career aspirations aren't just for you. Your success and happiness model the success and happiness you want your children to pursue when they're adults. In essence, when we rewrote that Sucky Song earlier, we were moving you a step closer to adopting a Model Mindset.

As I began making this shift in my own career, it started to manifest itself as one of the most impactful win-wins in my life. I recall one moment where I realized the power of modeling – for my children *and* for my employees.

We were prepping for our annual client conference, and since I was the CEO, I had a key role to play. Just a few weeks before the event I had an "Oh, shit!" moment. I realized the event overlapped with my daughter's tenth birthday. I remember saying to Ella, "I'm sorry, honey, I'm going to have to miss your birthday, but we'll make up for it over the weekend."

I sat in the guilt for a few days. And then it hit me – I didn't have to miss her birthday.

The conference was just a few hours' drive away, and its last day landed on Ella's birthday. I would drive back and get her so that she could attend the final event with me. Ella had never been to Boston, so her face lit up when I proposed the plan. We arrived just in time for the evening festivities at the iconic Cheers Bar. Everyone lit up when we walked in together; we were that evening's "Norm."

It was incredible. I introduced her to our clients and my colleagues. We got her a birthday cake, and she served it to everyone. And I still did business. I was able to connect with our clients on a whole new level now that they saw me as more than just a CEO. They saw me as a mom. As a human.

When I decided to bring her with me, I did it for Ella. But I also did it for myself. It was truly a selfish attempt at "having it all." What I didn't plan for, though, was what happened next. The most powerful outcome was when I received emails from people saying how inspiring it was for them to see me bring my daughter to the event. Many of our clients and employees were women, and they said it opened their eyes to how they, too, can create work-life balance. It showed them that there is often more than one solution to a problem.

People are inspired less by the words you say and more by the actions you display.

I've always been a strong advocate for having work-life balance, as make-me-want-to-puke cliché as that sounds. I'd been known to give more than a reasonable number of public service announcements to my team on things like focusing on family first and the importance of taking a *real* vacation. But I know that talk goes *whoooosh!* over people's heads if you don't demonstrate it yourself. People need to see and feel the permission you're trying to give them. Never underestimate the power of *show, don't tell.* When I appeared at the conference with Ella, it was more powerful than any memo, speech, or mandate I could have given.

Have you ever heard someone say, "I'm a visual learner?" They mean they absorb information better when it's supported by diagrams or a flowchart or something visual. But visual learning is much more than diagrams and arrows.

The best diagrams are in 3-D. The best diagram is you.

When I set out to write this book, I did what we all do with most things. I tried to do it with a Manage Mindset. I started working in 2-D. I worried about finding the perfect words, well-constructed stories, by the book (pun intended) grammar, and poetically descriptive sentences. But about a quarter of the way into my first draft, I realized *that* kind of language wasn't going to change your life. It might have made me look like a fancy writer, but this book needed to be less about choosing words that conveyed authenticity and more about feeling authentic. I needed to demonstrate authenticity, even when you didn't realize I was doing it. So, I scrapped the first draft of the book and started over because I wanted to be sure I modeled my message. I hope you can feel it.

Growth is driven 10% by what you learn and 90% by what you see.

What does this mean for you? How do you make use of this in your mission to present your authentically badass self to the world?

Be aware of what you are teaching or modeling every day – those may be tactical concepts, strongly held beliefs, or lessons you've learned. Here's a list of thought starters to help you shift from a Manage Mindset to a Model Mindset:

- Start exercising during lunch to show your employees/coworkers how important it is to find time to move.
- Raise your hand to lead a presentation you're deathly afraid to do, and then ask your children to help you prepare for it.
- (Really) disconnect when you go on vacation, sending a megaphone message to others to do the same.
- Ask quieter employees to weigh in during a meeting to demonstrate a company culture change you'd like to see. (Culture change should *always* be created through modeling!)
- Leave a job you're unhappy at to show your life partner they can do the same.
- In an interview, don't talk about how well you collaborate and connect with others, focus on actually connecting and collaborating with the interviewer.
- In a meeting, tell a story that brings to light a point you're trying to make.
- Lead a large meeting without a huge PowerPoint document, and you'll inspire others to do the same.
- Take your child(ren) with you to a work event.
- Don't just talk about authenticity, be authentic!

When you become aware of the power of modeling, you'll be amazed at how often you think about it. At work. At home. Everywhere.

In fact, just a few hours ago I took a break from writing and asked my kids to go on a walk with me. When we got back to the house, I was just about to kick off my sneakers without untying them. And then I stopped. I realized the little dude was right behind me. I hate when he does that. "You're going to ruin your shoes, Mick," I always say to him. I caught myself and instead, stopped, bent down, and untied my shoes.

I encourage you to put this Model Mindset into motion this week. What one or two situations can you think of where you can model instead of manage? A simple formula is to

- Think about what you want for someone else. What do you want their lives to be like? What energy do you want them to feel? How do you want them to act?
- And then reverse engineer it back to yourself. Demonstrate what you want them to have/be/do.

Give yourself the same compassion that you give to your best friend. Be a great leader at work by walking the walk. Show your children the kind of gutsy, free, balanced, successful, happy life you want them to have. Set yourself up for success by serving others with your actions.

And if nothing else, make this your new mantra ...

Don't give a damn if people forget your words, but damn it, never let them forget your actions.

21 Adapt: Plug and evolve

"Adapt what is useful, reject what is useless, and add what is specifically your own."

~ Bruce Lee - martial artist, actor, and someone who had a special gift of being able to Kung Fu both your body and your mind

Adapting seems to contradict the idea of being authentic, doesn't it?! You might be thinking, *If I adapt, doesn't that mean I'm no longer being authentic?*

I promise, it doesn't.

Adaptation is a critical element of strategically using your authenticity. Maybe even the most critical.

If you're worried that adapting will wipe out being who you really are, please don't fear. I'm going to walk you through the two parts of adaptation and help you see that adapting doesn't erode your authenticity, it enhances your connectivity. It also ensures that you are more focused on who you *want* to be in the future versus who you are today. Understanding the power of adaptation will remove some of the barriers that have held you back from fully unleashing the power of authenticity at work.

PLUGGING INTO OTHERS

The first part of adaptation requires you to be able to connect to, or plug into, other people's authenticity. This is where the expanded definition of authenticity is critical. It's not about just being yourself, remember? Without adaptation we would continuously bang our heads up against this quandary: If authenticity is just being yourself, how do you connect with people who aren't like you? For authenticity to benefit all of us, we can't simply be ourselves, we have to find a way to plug into others and fire up their authenticity too.

Did I lose you? Stay with me here.

Think about a time when you traveled to another country. If you're from the United States for example, you can't simply throw your blow dryer or electric shaver into your suitcase and expect to wake up and walk out onto the streets of Paris looking hot as shit. Why not? Because France's electrical outlets are different than the ones in the US. You have to adapt! It's no different with people. If we believe that connection is a critical byproduct of being more authentic, that means you have to carry around an *adapt*er kit and whip it out from time to time.

I know you feel like you're different than many people you work with. But trust me, they're feeling that too. Focus on meeting people halfway, whatever that might mean. Be sure to continue to be the same beautiful person you are. I want you to show more of who you are. At the same time, you also need to observe those around you, understand how they operate, and what lights them up. If they have a tough exterior, where do you see small signs of opportunity that you can plug into?

*****IMPORTANT NOTE: This does *not* mean you should succumb to the boring, snoozy fakeness of the current corporate world. This means that you should plug your authenticity into others and charge them up.*****

One day I was talking to my podcast co-host, Nicole. During our *b Cause podcast*, I often coach her real-time and really authentically, through her work challenges. Recently we spoke about her desire for a promotion. We were working together on how to pitch to her boss, and I reminded Nicole to be ready for a common reaction: the exorcism. That is, most managers tend to first think *no* when challenged or asked for something big. They say no because if they immediately say yes, especially as it relates to something that costs significant money, they might miss something they should have thought of and the no protects them.

I warned her that her manager's first reaction would likely be an "I don't think so," and suggested she prepare to let him have the time and space to express all the reasons her idea wasn't a good one (and defend himself for not having thought of it himself). "Wait it out," I told Nicole. This is an important strategy, and not just when pitching a promotion.

Several months later, Nicole got that promotion. While reflecting, she reminded me about the exorcism coaching and how it helped her during that promotion discussion and again in another work situation. Nicole had raised something a bit controversial with her manager. She said to me, "Because of you, I now recognize the 'exorcism' he needs to have first and to let it pass. I no longer go immediately into defend mode. I wait it out. And once I can see that he's gotten through that, then I push on the points I want to make." She approached the situation with her boss differently. She learned how to better adapt and plug into her boss. And it made a huge difference in the outcome.

These patterns are everywhere. Start becoming curious about how you can stay true to who you are, while also finding a connection to someone else's authenticity. Whatever you do, stop believing that you can't be successful because those "above you" have different plugs than you do. Of course, they do! A big reason theirs are different is because the people that came before them had different plugs too. You can shape the plugs of others. Because authenticity is contagious. When you're authentic, you're able to shape the brass plugs around you. The top-brass personalities aren't permanent. They are evolving. And no matter where you sit in the organization, you can help them evolve to find their best, authentic selves.

YOUR OWN AUTHENTIC ADAPTATION

Everyone has talents, good things about them. But you can't remain who you are. Yes, that's right. Your underlying traits, beliefs, and quirks will remain with you until the day you die, but your authentic self should always be evolving. (It's called growth.) This is the second part of adaptation.

Organizational psychologist and author, Dr. Benjamin Hardy, writes in his book *Personality Isn't Permanent* that we've been hamstrung by things like personality tests (Myers-Briggs, Enneagram, and the like). These tests, he argues, actually hold us back from becoming the person we ultimately could be. Hardy makes the case for your authentic self to be in a constant state of growth and evolution — that we should be continually working to define who we want to become.

Taking this a step further, Dan Gilbert, Harvard psychologist and author of *Stumbling on Happiness*, talks about a major misconception many people have, which psychologists call "the end of history illusion," his own version of a Sucky Song. This is when people believe that who they are at that very moment is their final being. Even people who have experienced significant personal growth in the past often don't believe they'll continue to change that way in the future. Gilbert says, "Human beings are works in progress that mistakenly think they're finished."

Wowzer.

Lesson here: Please stop walking around spending most of your time trying to find your authentic self. Instead, focus more on defining who you want your future self to be.

I see so much written and talked about in the realm of "finding who you are." While it's important to know what has shaped you so far, simply finding who you are will never leave you satisfied. Like Monty Python looking for the Holy Grail, it's likely you'll be clicking those coconuts together forever. If instead you stop looking for that Holy Grail and focus more on the authentic person you *want* to be, you'll be amazed at how quickly you'll arrive there.

Every so often, I write what I call a Future Diary. I sit down and type out a day in the future, as if it's just happened. I always start with "I woke up in the morning and ..." and write the most fantastical account of who I am and what I got to do on that perfect day. I wrote my first Future Diary when I was still in my corporate job, detailing a day one year in the future and how I felt after telling people I was leaving. I wrote about the things I desired most in my next chapter, with no detail too small. For example, one of the most important things was having the ability to wake up at 7:00 am (not at 5:00 am like I had for the past ten years!) and snuggle with my husband. Less than a year later, I had retired from my job and nearly everything in my Future Diary came true.

So, I decided to write another, again about a day one year in the future. I typed away about how I had just given a keynote speech and the exhilaration I felt from doing that. A few months later, I was asked to give a keynote speech to about six hundred people at our local theater (and completely unsolicited by me!). I also wrote down, for the first time, that I wanted to host a podcast with my friend Nicole, something she and I had never spoken about. But here's the magic-not-really-magic: Once you write something down, your brain starts to think, *Hmm, well, I guess I could take a small step towards making that happen.* A month or so later I proposed the podcast to Nicole. We're now approaching one hundred episodes. And look, did everything come true? Nope. But because I dreamed big, that doesn't matter. I was still able to become a new Erin who was beyond my wildest dreams.

My latest Future Diary is written as if the day happened in May of 2025. The things I'm doing, the people I'm influencing, the person I've become is almost ridiculous. But I know that at least 50% of it will happen. In fact, one of the things I wrote was that I'd do a TEDx Talk. A month later, I was selected to give a talk at TEDx Farmingdale. By focusing on and writing down who I want to be in the future, I am continually adapting my authenticity to ensure I become my highest, truest self.

Adaptation allows you to stay true to your soul while also fueling your soul for more.

I highly encourage you to take up this practice. Nearly everyone I coach has written their own Future Diary. Start by writing what happened on a day one year from now. Not a list but an actual story … a diary entry. This exercise will allow you to create a version of yourself that is beyond your wildest dreams. It gives you a clear view into future you. And then simply say, "Hmm, what one step can I take to adapt myself, to get closer to that amazing new version of me?" And dream big! I always encourage people to make it about 50% accurate. It should be indulgent, fanciful, and audacious. Then, even if you get only halfway there, holy shit, your new self will be beyond anything you could dream of if you were simply focused on understanding who you are today.

Development demands discomfort

As you start to write your Future Diary and focus on your future self, here's a warning: You're going to have to get uncomfortable. I want to ensure you're adapting and evolving at work in a way that ensures you attain the success you crave.

Remember when I was offered that job in the international division that I felt highly unqualified for? When I first started, I tapped into some of the things I already knew how to do. I held a meeting with people who I knew would have great input into our strategy. I hired a consultant to help do a small project. But other than those few things, I had no clue what I was doing.

But the reality is, when you take on something new and uncomfortable, you know the first few steps to take. You know that if you take those steps, you'll start to figure out the things you don't know how to do. All you need to do is open one curtain at a time. And then sure as heck, the next curtain will be sitting behind that first one. If I could point to just one factor that led to the success I've had, it would be that I embraced the discomfort of growth. It was those really uncomfortable assignments and new jobs that catapulted my career. I want you to do the same. I want you to adopt what I call The 50% Rule.

THE 50% RULE:
Take on each new assignment, role, or job only if it'll make you 50% uncomfortable.

Essentially, look for "what's next" — where about half of the work will make great use of your experience while the other half scares the shit out of you.

Every ... single ... time ... you get the itch to do something new, hold on to this rule.

If you want more, then you need to apply this rule. So often I talk with people who are yearning to get the VP role, have a more influential position, get the raise, make an impact ... whatever it is. But as they seek out "what's next?" they take roles that are a step here or a step there. Instead, I encourage them (and you) to look for leaps. Ask yourself, *Will this make me 50% uncomfortable?* If the answer is no, then I can almost guarantee it won't get you any closer to your ultimate goal.

Now, if you're thinking, *But, uh, isn't it nearly impossible to get hired into those roles?* The answer is *nope*. Nearly every new job I took fit this test. I've also coached several people who have changed their mindset and applied this rule. And guess what? They got the 50% uncomfortable job.

But if you're still leery, then I suggest you start by applying this rule *within* your current job. For example, raise your hand for an assignment that meets this rule. Explain to your manager that you're willing to figure things out. Experiment with leading a project that's not in your job description. Fight through the blind spots and the unknowns, and at the other end of that will be something magical: a new and improved you.

Adaptation is about connection and energy and growth. Adaptation isn't about changing who you are to fit a mold. It's about evolving who you are to be bolder. Your willingness to adapt helps you shine a light on another person so you can see their authentic self. It helps you shine your own spotlight on yourself, so others can see you. And it helps you see your future self when there are shadows and blind spots. You are a beautiful soul. It's time to shine a light on you.

Your success is in your control if you're brave enough to feel out of control.

Your success is
in your control
if you're brave
enough to feel out
of control.

22 Narrate: Wake them up before they go-go

"The most powerful person in the world is the storyteller."

~ Steve Jobs - business magnate and someone who knew what he was talking about

As I've mentioned, my father is a storytelling junkie. He showed me the power of story when he was a teacher but he also proved that it wasn't just a tactic for those at the front of the classroom. My father retired from teaching and began his second-half career as a real estate agent. While selling houses is a far cry from teaching algebra, he uses the same strategy: Connect with people through authenticity. And a big part of authenticity is not interacting with someone by talking facts but instead bringing all of yourself through the power of story.

Now, I wish I could say that my father's experience is where I learned the power of storytelling in the business world, but the truth is, my reverence for using stories in *business* came from a different man: Tommy Boy.

Yes, *that* Tommy Boy. Chris Farley. One of the funniest comedians to ever walk this earth. And in his movie *Tommy Boy,* he teaches us that stories, not facts, are the key to success. (If you haven't seen this movie, put down this book and watch it immediately.)

Even if you've seen it, you may remember the laughs more than the lesson. Let me just remind you of Tommy Callahan's important revelation that he was handling the family business all wrong.

After Tommy inherits Callahan Auto Parts, he teams up with Richard (played by David Spade), a Callahan company veteran, to save the business. When Tommy first starts his journey, he handles it like most people would. He sits in office after office and gives customers facts and figures about why Callahan Auto Parts makes better brake pads than its competitors. And he gets rejection after rejection.

Then Tommy starts to uncover the power of storytelling. Does it magically solve his issues and turn the company around? Nope. But he keeps at it, refining his story. For example, he attempts to demonstrate the importance of their high-quality brake pads using toy cars, which leads to the cars being lit on fire. While I commend his creativity and use of story, we all learn that lighting a potential customer's desk toys on fire is going a bit too far.

Tommy finally has an epiphany when he and Richard are at a diner. Tommy wants some chicken wings, but the waitress, Helen, informs him the kitchen is closed until dinner. He decides to bring Helen up to speed on his troubles, explaining to her why he sucks at sales. "Let's say I go into some guy's office. Let's say he's even remotely interested in buying something. Well then, I get all excited. I'm like Joe-Joe the idiot circus boy with a pretty new pet. The pet is my possible new sale." His dinner roll becomes the prop for this pet/possible sale that he ends up obliterating. He says to Helen, "That's when people like us gotta forge ahead. Am I right, Helen?"

But guess what happens? Despite Helen holding her ground earlier about the kitchen being closed, she agrees to go back to the kitchen herself and drop in some chicken wings for Tommy. And that's when it hits both he and Richard. Richard says to him, "That one-eighty you just pulled on the waitress. Why can't you sell like that?" Richard tells him that he got the "sale" (the wings) because Tommy relaxed and did what his father did so well – read people, understood what they want, and gave it to them through storytelling.

(If you want the full scene, it's much funnier than I can describe. Just search "Why I suck as a salesperson" on YouTube.)

While Tommy found his way through trial and error, the neuroscience behind the power of storytelling is compelling. Cognitive psychologist Jerome Bruner is well known for his research into storytelling. His data suggests that people remember stories twenty-two times more than they recall data and facts. In a world of distraction, increasing someone's ability to recall what you said by 2200% is pretty darned compelling.

But we aren't setting out simply to be memorable. We're on a journey to use the power of authenticity to create stronger connections and get better results ... at work and in life. So, what else is it about storytelling that makes it a more powerful way to connect?

Well, first, data is boring, but listening to a story immediately ignites curiosity as you wait to hear how all the pieces come together. But there's actually a scientific explanation for the power a story has to create stronger connections. If you recall, earlier when I talked about the business case for authenticity, I noted the importance that oxytocin plays in creating trust. The same Harvard professor, Paul Zak, who helped us build the case for authenticity, did a study that found oxytocin levels rise when people listen to a story. Furthermore, a person's oxytocin levels were directly related to how willing they were to help another person or organization. Storytelling triggers a release of oxytocin, which we know is an indicator of increased trust. That trust opens the way to create greater connection.

Do you ever have these frustrations?

- I work so hard, but I just can't get people to do what I need them to do to get the job done.
- People don't seem to understand what I'm saying to them.
- I get so annoyed when people don't pay attention to what I'm saying in meetings.
- I feel invisible to leaders in the organization.
- I can't seem to connect with certain people.

Telling stories can be a nearly immediate solution to these challenges. When you start to incorporate stories into your work and interactions, people will pause, be curious, and feel more connected to you.

Storytelling turns distraction into attraction.

I use stories all the time in place of facts and figures. Even when it feels a bit awkward to do so. I recall one big meeting I had with my boss' boss and her leadership team. It was month two of my interim CEO status, and my business unit was summoned to present at a meeting in front of the leadership team of our parent company. The company I led managed financial health care accounts (if you live in the US you probably know our main product as a Health Savings Account). I was about ten minutes into my presentation and a small debate arose. The president of the enterprise made the argument that people who were more highly educated understood how a Health Savings Account (HSA) worked much better than those who were less educated.

While it seemed like a sensible assumption, the data we had from numerous studies showed that this wasn't the case. In fact, most people, regardless of education, don't understand that an HSA is actually designed to help you save for medical expenses in retirement.

When she hit me with this inaccurate assumption, I had two options:

Option A: Annoy her with boring stats that would essentially tell her *you're wrong.*

Option B: Tell her a story to illustrate my point.

I opted for B. I told her and the entire room:

> Just a few weeks ago I was in a meeting with one of the company's head actuaries. As we were talking about Health Savings Accounts, I asked him about his personal interactions with his own HSA. When I asked him if he saved his HSA for future medical expenses, he responded, "No, we always use it immediately for our medical expenses."

> Then, just a few days later, I was driving in the car with my seven-year-old daughter. Out of the blue she asked me, "Mommy, if you had a million dollars, what five things would you do with it?" I went through my list of five things. Then I asked Ella what five things she would do with her money. She responded, "One — toys. Two — clothes. Three — charity. Four — a boat. Five — I'd save some money in case I had an unexpected medical emergency." So, I really don't believe there's a correlation between education and people's understanding of HSAs.

I think everyone was a little stunned. They certainly weren't on their phones and tablets. They found themselves drawn into the story. And they couldn't help but smile and nod. Instead of arguing a point with data and facts, I took them on a journey with a story.

I get it. For most people this feels awkward and complex. No worries. I'll coach you through this, step by step. Before you know it, you'll be a storytelling machine. Much like we did with the Sucky Songs though, we first need to prime you by removing any limiting beliefs, or Storytelling Roadblocks, you might think are in your way.

Storytelling Roadblocks

When you think about the concept of storytelling, do any of these roadblocks pop up for you?

- My colleagues are going to think I'm weird.
- I don't have any tragic stories.

- Storytelling is only for extroverted people.
- I'm not funny enough to be a storyteller.
- Telling a story will take up too much time.
- Telling stories is only for the "big stage," and I don't hang out there.

Let's break each one of these down:

1. **My colleagues are going to think I'm weird.** Your colleagues are actually going to think you're the coolest cat in town. In a *New York Times* article, Annie Murphy Paul points to the numerous studies showing that, when you tell a story, people actually place themselves right into the story you're telling, as if they are with you. Essentially, they *aren't* listening to your story, they're experiencing it. They'll be so drawn in that they'll likely be stripped of many, if not all, of their brain waves that make them all judgy-judgy. (This last part is highly unscientific research on my part.)
2. **I don't have any tragic stories.** I was once coaching someone on a presentation she was giving to a large town hall meeting. When I urged her to start it with a story, she said, "But I don't have anything tragic that happened in my life." I explained that tragedy isn't a story requirement. I encouraged her to draw on where her passion for the topic came from. She decided to share a story about her mother having worked for the same company for over thirty years, and because of that, she found her own calling for the work. She told this story to kick off her presentation, and she told me afterward that it was one of the proudest moments of her life.

3. **Storytelling is only for extroverted people.** Telling stories is actually a great strategy for introverts. While it may feel a bit out of the norm at first, when you tell a story, it doesn't just draw in your audience, it also puts you into your own flow. I often start sections in this book with a story for just that reason. It's partly strategic, to help you understand my point via a metaphor or a tangible example. But I also do it to get into my own flow, so that I can more easily articulate what I'm trying to get across to you. My words always seem to come more easily after I write a story. Turning a fact-based conversation into a story will help you move right into flow, which is where we all do our best work. Hey, you might find so much flow that you even forget you're an introvert.
4. **I'm not funny enough to be a storyteller.** Remember what I said about humor being the salt and pepper to being authentic? Sure, things almost always taste better with salt and pepper, but I don't want you to give up cooking because you don't have salt and pepper on hand. Humor often pokes its little nose into stories when you least expect it. You can also add humility or unexpectedness as a substitute for humor. It's like adding butter when the recipe calls for Crisco. The cookies taste amazing either way!
5. **Telling a story will take up too much time.** This is one of the biggest misconceptions. You think people don't have time to listen to your story. This barricade is likely why youtalksuperfastinmeetingstobesureyoudonttakeuptoomu-chofpeoplestime. Guess what, they didn't actually process a thing you said. People don't get frustrated when you *take*

up their time. People get frustrated when you *waste* their time. Think about this. Would you rather watch a five-minute shitty show or a thirty-minute nail-biter?

6. **Telling stories is only for the "big stage," and I don't hang out there.** This one's a no-brainer: You need to tell stories when giving a presentation. But that's just the tip of the iceberg. Stories can be told ANYWHERE. And they can be culled out of many different scenarios. This is where we'll head next. I want to be sure you see that stories can exponentially improve your connections at work ... and your career overall.

I hope this helps you see that telling stories isn't as scary as you might have thought and you're at least curious enough to take the next step with me. Okay? Good. In this next section, I'm going to talk about the many places you can start incorporating storytelling. I'll also walk you through the Five Story Inventory so you can easily substitute my stories for your own.

STORY NEIGHBORHOODS

Here are some of the many places where you can incorporate a story:

- presenting at a town hall
- leading off a meeting
- one-on-one with your boss
- at a team meeting
- in a sales meeting
- in a customer meeting

- on your LinkedIn profile (check out mine @Erin Hatzikostas if you want inspiration — all my job descriptions are mini-stories)
- in your out-of-office message

And, as with just about everything I teach in *You Do You(ish)*, you can apply this technique outside of work too. You might use a story to explain something to your child or if you're arguing a point with your spouse. A story is also useful when trying to explain what you do for a living.

Now, I know what you might be thinking. Isn't telling a story in a one-on-one meeting with my boss or an out-of-office message a bit too dramatic? No. Stories are a great way to capture people's attention or help them understand a point you're making.

Stories are also extremely powerful for your resumé and everything you do on LinkedIn. For example, instead of starting your LinkedIn post with "I was so honored to speak at blah-diddy-blah," tell them a story about how you got involved with the organization or a story that inspired your talk. I guarantee your engagement will skyrocket. I can't think of any story that wouldn't work both on stage, sitting in a fifty-square-foot office, or in a 140-character tweet.

Stop telling *snoozy* facts and start telling *doozy* stories.

I know this is a lot to take in. If you're at least saying, "Well, okay … maybe," then let's get a bit more tangible and specific because my primary goal here is to open your mind to the possibilities and have you start by replacing one snoozy fact in the next few weeks with a story. In order to kick-start this process, I'll give you five different types of stories you can tell. Then, I'll have you get your hands dirty and start writing down some ideas to get your storytelling party started.

STORY INVENTORY: FIVE DIFFERENT TALE TYPES

I've spent a lifetime telling stories. But becoming a good storyteller is no different than learning anything new; it's all about practice, practice, practice. I want to help you start practicing by leveraging what I call the STORY Inventory. This framework will give you a solid foundation for your storytelling practice. And ultimately, telling stories will help you gain people's attention, stand out, and be seen as a leader!

S = **S**imiles.

Using a simile is like giving milk to a baby. See what I did there? :-) Yes, metaphors and analogies are a form of story and are helpful when you're trying to explain complex information. For example, my team would often get frustrated that we weren't investing enough in new technology. I would say to them, "Business is like playing chess. If we could just take our king, queen, knight, and pawn and smash them across the table and knock all our opponent's pieces down, we would. But instead, business is about figuring out which chess piece to move first, and then next. It's all about trade-offs and strategically investing in the right places at the right time." That analogy always seemed to really stick with people. It helped them understand that we couldn't always do the things that seemed obvious. It was like chess. We had to move one piece at a time.

T = **T**weets.

This is another method for telling your story, believe it or not. I've replaced the old crusty "elevator pitch" with the more modern version of that – the verbal "tweet." For example, several years ago we had just finished up a two-and-a-half-day leadership summit for the company I was leading. That afternoon I had to present at our quarterly business review for the CEO of Aetna. As I was putting together notes for my update, I was torn about whether I should talk about the leadership summit. On one hand, it was a huge turning point for our company, so I couldn't imagine not talking about it. But he was a busy guy, running a ginormous corporation. Did he really care about this fluffy stuff? I decided to "split the baby in half" and give him a verbal tweet. I updated him on the numbers and sales info as usual, and then I added, "And we also just finished holding a leadership summit. It was the proudest two-and-a-half days of my career." I realized, he needed to know we did something profound. But he didn't need to know *what* we did. He simply needed to *feel* it. Most of the time, simply giving someone the tweetable version is more impactful than a list of whos, whats, and wheres. And this is especially true when communicating with executives. Here's a rule to live by: Respond to a big question with a small story.

O = **O**ther people's stories.

Stories do not have to be our own. In fact, telling someone else's stories is a great way to draw people in and make a fresh point. An example from my personal story inventory comes from a time we had our annual planning meeting. I was sick of the usual 120-line operating plans, in which we always set ourselves up for failure. I wanted to take a different approach and have each leader pick just one obsession for them and their team to focus on. As we gathered around the table, I decided that instead of kicking off with the normal pomp and circumstance, I'd tell someone else's story:

In 1919, two explorers, Robert Falcon Scott and Roald Amundsen, each aimed to be the first to make it to the South Pole. Team Scott was ambitious – they not only wanted to reach the South Pole but wanted to focus on science as well. They were the most heavily resourced, with several tools and methods of transportation to reach their destination. Team Amundsen, on the other hand, was focused solely on reaching their destination, and used only dogs to help them.

Both teams had similar regimens to prepare for their voyage, with the mindset that they needed to walk twenty miles a day. But each team approached this differently. When there was inclement weather, Team Scott would go a shorter distance; when there was better weather, they would go farther. On the other hand, Team Amundsen always went twenty miles, no matter the weather. In the end, Team Amundsen made it to the South Pole. Team Scott perished trying.

The story demonstrated the importance of focus, of picking one strategy and sticking with it. I wanted to provoke a new mindset that would be a departure from that of the year before, which was "Do it all." By telling this story, I sent a permanent mark straight to their brains — that we were going to do things differently this year.

R = **R**elate.

Good storytelling is about putting yourself knee-deep in a situation, allowing you to give people an experience instead of a lecture. These work really well in sales. So many times, salespeople talk about this widget or that feature. They put 2-D words on a PowerPoint slide. And then they wonder why they didn't make the sale. People buy with their hearts and guts, not their brains. Appeal to their hearts and guts with a story that they can see themselves in. If possible, tell a story about your experience using a product, and how the different features you offer made a difference. Or maybe even more impactful, tell a story from a customer's perspective. Of course, it's commonplace to gather testimonials from clients. But those aren't the real gold. The real gold comes when a customer tells a story about their experience and how their life changed as a result. If I were in sales, I'd spend 90% of my time mining that gold. Finding and spending it is the fastest way to make a sale.

Y = **Y**ours.

Last but not least, tell your own stories! Again, an impactful story doesn't have to be dramatic, funny, or profound. It simply needs to help you twist the listener's brain ninety degrees and point it toward the semi-hypnotic trance that brings them on a journey with you. Nothing is too trite! For example, the other day I was talking to a potential investor for a company of which I am a board member. Our product, a telehealth solution for back and spine care, is different from the competition because we work with people before they get to the acute-pain stage. I told the group of investors a story about how that morning I was in our garden weeding. I related the concept of weeding from the roots versus just plucking the plant from the top to what our company's solution provides. Not dramatic. Not fancy. Not funny. Just effective.

MINING FOR STORY GOLD

Stories are all around you.

You know what it's like when you decide on the next car you want to buy? You suddenly see that car everywhere. If you open your mind to the concept that stories are gold, you'll start gathering a treasure trove. They are in books, podcasts, and movies. There are huge dramatic stories, like the South Pole explorers. And there are everyday moments, like pulling weeds from your garden.

One question you might have is, How do I know which stories to use? Well, I've found that most stories have multiple (three to five) conclusions that can be drawn from them, so I've used the same story several times, making different points each time I tell it. For example, the story I told you about my son and I riding our bikes in Vermont can be used to indicate that there are multiple paths to take but also to make a point about the power of curiosity. Or I can use it to derive a point about leadership.

For that reason, I suggest that you start by creating a library of stories. It doesn't have to be fancy. Just a place where you log stories you've told over the years. You can also write down things that happen every day and draw from them whenever you need to.

You can use these questions to prompt your thinking:

- What funny things did your kids say recently?
- What stories do your parents tell time and time again about you?
- What are some of your favorite stories from books you've read? (Hint: Write these down when you're reading them.)
- What's a story about something you've overcome?
- What's one of the most embarrassing things that's happened to you at work? Or the biggest mistake you've made?
- What are some everyday things you do that parallel complex things you do at work?
- What's the funniest story you tell friends over drinks? (Mine's a story about the first time my husband and I kissed. It didn't make the cut for this book but I've told it a few times on Instagram. It's ROFL material!)

The process will be a bit messy at first. You'll likely drop this chapter like a mic, tell a killer story in a meeting, and feel like a superhero. And the next day, as you go back to pounding away at your keyboard, getting more and more entranced by the "clear your email game," hopping from meeting to meeting without time to pee, you'll slide back into your old ways. You'll get lured back to normalcy by all those snoozy people around you. Understand, that's okay. I want to simply encourage you to get addicted to something new. Addicted to the feeling that comes with storytelling. Addicted to the smiles you'll get from people as you take them on a journey. Addicted to people listening to what you have to say. Addicted to continually looking for another parallel, another way to take people into an experience with you instead of dragging them through flatlining information. And detoxing from snooziness and getting addicted to dooziness takes time and practice. It won't be a straight line. It will be a ... journey.

It helps to have this simple archive of story material saved somewhere. It's not just about the stories themselves; this list will also serve as a constant reminder that you're resolved to become a storytelling machine. Keep at it. Be kind to yourself when a story doesn't quite stick. Continue to practice.

Promise me that in the next week you'll tell one story where you normally would have snoozed people with big words and data. The following week I want you to tell two stories. The week after that, three. In a month or so, the training wheels will naturally fall off and you'll be a storytelling master.

I can't wait to hear your stories.

• • • • • • •

Your life is a collection of stories. Tell them.

• • • • • • • •

Results trump ridiculousness

I went on to get that CEO position … and I became the proud "owner" of a bit of a shitshow. The company had been struggling for a long time. Bogged down by a tough few years integrating into its new parent company, operations had been very messy, earnings hadn't grown in four years, and employee morale was (rightfully so) pretty low.

After clocking small and large successes by using my authenticity as my new secret weapon, my authenticity was now on autopilot. For me, it was the only way to be (and to lead the company).

I told stories about my children at town halls. I danced with people on the front lines. I involved myself in the pick-up after food gatherings. And I never, EVER let emails go out that started with "On behalf of Erin Hatzikostas …" (I even wrote my own organizational announcements, removing my stupid headshot from the top of the email … everyone knew what the hell I looked like!)

What happened next was no miracle. People started to follow. People started to seek jobs within our organization. People got fired up and were relieved to be led by someone who wasn't stuffy, egotistical, or unapproachable.

And the results were the trump card to all my authentic audacity. Year after year, our earnings significantly increased. And not coincidentally, employee engagement scores and overall morale followed.

After leading the company for three years, our flat earnings turned into millions of dollars (tripling in just three years). Our culture index, measured each year by one of those industrial-strength HR surveys, went up twelve percentage points. Most importantly, employees were happy. And they were proud.

And me? I got to stay married. My kids thrived. I ran my half marathon personal best (still to this day). And I stayed … me.

This just might have been my best business case ever. Take that, actuarial exams.

23

Spark: Let's light some shit on fire!

"You know you're a good leader when people follow you out of curiosity."

~ Colin Powell - American politician, retired four-star army general, and total badass

We talked earlier about the contagious nature of authenticity, and how, when you start acting more authentic, you unlock this dormant power that's inside of you … and inside of others. We went on to talk about the authentic "yawns" that happen and how you can create that same contagion for others to bring out their authenticity.

In this final section on the Six Principles of Strategic Authenticity, I want to talk about sparking, or inspiring, others. This final component is the fuel that keeps your entire strategy going. I want to help you think about inspiration in a new way.

I was about two years into being the CEO when I received our annual employee survey results. The company was turning around — financials were soaring and my leadership team was energized and humming. I couldn't wait to dive into the survey results. *What a joyous place I'm creating,* I thought. Surely, I would be rewarded with reading hours of comments that put into words what I believed was happening – all the people were skipping into work, happy as could be.

Yeah, not so much.

I started looking at the numbers. Yes, the needle had moved. But I was disappointed to see that the results had only inched up from previous years. I decided to skip right past the numbers and go to the comments. Once I began reading the thirty-five pages of written comments, I was sure that HR had given me the wrong report. Despite the financial turnaround and the positive energy I was witnessing, there was still a lot of work to be done. Many people were frustrated by the lack of change on their teams. There were leadership issues. There were process issues. There were still a lot of unhappy people. I realized that what I saw on a daily basis was only the tip of the iceberg. There was still much work to do.

I was deflated. I'd worked my butt off, running around inspiring the shit out of people. I'd traveled to all of our offices across the country, put new protocols in place, led our town hall meetings in an energetic way that had never been done before. I'd been leading the company like an authentic Energizer Bunny. Why oh why were so many people still so miserable?! My inspiration fuel tank was empty. *Shit. What do I do now?!*

A few months later, I was presenting at an annual internal conference we held for people on our customer-facing teams. We had about two hundred people gathered for two days. As I was on stage giving my presentation, I could see a sparkle in their eyes. Even though that survey wasn't showing the progress I wanted, I could feel an energy shift. There was a feeling of pride that I hadn't seen in years. It was at that moment that I thought, *If we could get to a better culture almost by luck, what would happen if we actually tried to be great?* I decided then and there that we would make "creating a culture to be envied" our top priority. We would invest in it like it was a new product. We would put it at the center of our company strategy. It would be our differentiator.

Now, this isn't a book on leadership or culture, so I'm not going to bore you with the details on what we did next. (If you want more details on the cultural transformation we went through, check out the article I wrote for Business Insider, "3 'culture change' steps I made as a CEO that helped triple our earnings and increase our company culture score by 15%.") But I want to tell you about the most profound thing I learned when we decided to dive headfirst into the deep end of leadership and culture change.

As a leader, your job isn't to inspire people. Your job is to create an inspiration platform.

What I had misunderstood, until I saw those survey results, was that inspiration isn't just top-down. Inspiration comes from all directions, and I'd been focusing on just one of those directions. I thought my job as the CEO was to be the inspiration master. And what those employee survey results told me was that no matter how inspiring you are (or I was), inspirational reach can only go so far.

Instead, it was my job to create a Viral Inspiration Platform, a VIP.

My job was to make small sparks and focus on creating an environment that ensured people inspired each other. Does that make sense? Instead of focusing on inspiring others, I needed to create ways for others to inspire each other. That also meant I had to learn when to inspire and when to just get the eff out of the way.

When I finally realized this, I sparked simple changes that led to enormous flames. One of the simplest and most impactful things I did was to add an agenda item to the beginning of every staff meeting I led: "Slow down and inspire." This was awkward at first, but it changed everything for the better. Instead of jumping into issues and business items, we spent the first ten to fifteen minutes of each meeting sharing inspiring items. Initially, most people shared leadership best practices that they or someone on their team had done. But it quickly expanded to people sharing inspiration more broadly, like stories of team members who had lost 100 pounds, stories about running a first half marathon, stories about their child's big accomplishment.

This spark spread like wildfire. Soon there were little fires everywhere. Some leaders created themes for the meetings, like Motivational Monday and Fun Friday. Teams led by folks several levels below me were creating their own vision boards. Others started book clubs, where they read a book each month and then talked about it at their team meeting.

I knew something monumental had happened when I was regularly sitting in on meetings and feeling like a shitty leader. These people were talking about new ways they were inspiring each other and leading their teams, and I was like, *Damn, I suck.*

These guys are way better leaders than I've ever been. Seriously, if you want to know you're nailing it as a leader ... sit in on your own team meeting, and if you leave with the feeling that your employees are now leading WAY better than you are, that's when you can say: "Mic drop!"

That was the ultimate gold star for me. I had created a Viral Inspiration Platform.

Now, I'm sure you're thinking, *WTF, my boss is an asshole and would never do something like this!* The point here is a Viral Inspiration Platform is built by the collective. Hear me loud and clear on this: inspiration flows from *all* directions. It comes from people with "leader" in their title and from those without it. On a daily basis, I was inspired a thousand times more by people who reported under me than those who reported above me.

I was sparked by the surveys and others were sparked by something another person said or did. Inspiration isn't linear—there's no one starting point. It comes from everywhere and everyone. Inspiration is less like a backyard fire and more like fireworks, where the fire erupts simultaneously in all directions.

Stop waiting for your boss to give you permission. Stop waiting for the word "manager" or "leader" to be in your title to inspire others.

• • • • • • •

At any given moment, you have one of two jobs. To inspire or to be inspired.

• • • • • • • •

If you're not feeling inspired, it's *your* job to go out and seek inspiration. You're doing that now by reading this book. Once you're inspired, it's *your* job to go out and inspire others.

You're not always going to get handed inspiration on a cute little sparkler stick. Inspiration is push and pull. Think of it as a game of Hot Potato – as soon as you get it, you have to throw it to somebody else. And of course, inspiration isn't always obvious. Remember my "Path B" introduction when we talked about using humility? I told the story of my friend, Amy, coming home from class, excited to tell me about the career she found for me. Well, if you take that story further, you'll see that she didn't just inspire my career. You see, if I'd never tried to become an actuary, I would never have moved from Michigan to Connecticut. I wouldn't have met my husband. And I would not have my children, Ella and Mick.

It's heavy shit. I know. This is the power of inspiration.

Amy wasn't my boss or parent. Amy simply found the inspiration Hot Potato and threw it to the next person, me! By tossing me that bad boy, she changed the trajectory of not just my career but my life.

I hadn't seen Amy in twenty years when I travelled to Florida for a work gathering. I posted my travel plans on Facebook (something I very rarely do), and Amy saw I'd be nearby where she lived, so we made plans to meet up. I'd had the epiphany a few years earlier that her suggestion had tilted the trajectory of my entire adult life. But I had never told her that. We sat down for dinner, excited to catch up. I don't think she saw what was coming. I reflected on that moment – one that she barely remembered – and told her how profoundly she had changed my life with that one dose of inspiration.

I tear up every time I tell this story, including writing this now. I've since told this to hundreds of people. This story even helped my children to appreciate how precious life is, and it also showed them the power of inspiration.

We've spent a lot of time going through the Six Principles of Strategic Authenticity. I hope you see that it's *all* just one big inspirational flywheel. It's about digging deep and doubling down. And when you start to do that – even just practicing a little bit, day by day – you'll be sparking that same change in those around you. An authentic yawn is the best way to start inspiring others to do the same. Yawn a little more each day and then don't forget to peek around you. Watch how your peers start to do the same. Get excited when your team starts to be even more authentic than you are. Laugh a little evil laugh when you see your authenticity rubbing off on the asshole boss. Rejoice when you see your kids being more authentic.

I truly believe that the best way to move forward is to be inspired by the joy you bring to others. That's certainly what's helped me write over fifty thousand words in this book, when I could barely write a five-page paper as a math major in college. You have no idea how much you (yes, you) inspired this book. The times we spent in my office, hearing your frustrations. The times we went to lunch and you said, "You know Erin, I'm good where I'm at." The late-night phone calls when you were fucking burnt toast from work and I had to help you put some peanut butter on your wounds. The comments you had on a podcast episode we did. The LinkedIn private message that told me to keep going … that what I was saying mattered. The coaching calls that made me realize there were new Sucky Songs being sung that I hadn't even heard before. The amazing, brilliant ideas you've shared. The ballsy moves you've made. The shit you've accomplished at work that I would have no idea how to begin. Your expression of creativity through the spoken and written words. You are inspiring me and inspiring others every day.

Inspiration is the intangible energy that keeps us all going. When you help others tune out Sucky Songs and instead tune in to the station that is jamming some Beyoncé or Bob Marley or Eminem, amazing shit happens. When you help others tune in, you get to dance alongside them. It's not a one-person party. This book isn't a solo adventure. Your life isn't a solitary mountain climb. It's a fucking dance party. And you can invite whoever you want, whenever you want. Just be sure to dance, even where you're not supposed to.

Six Principles of Strategic Authenticity

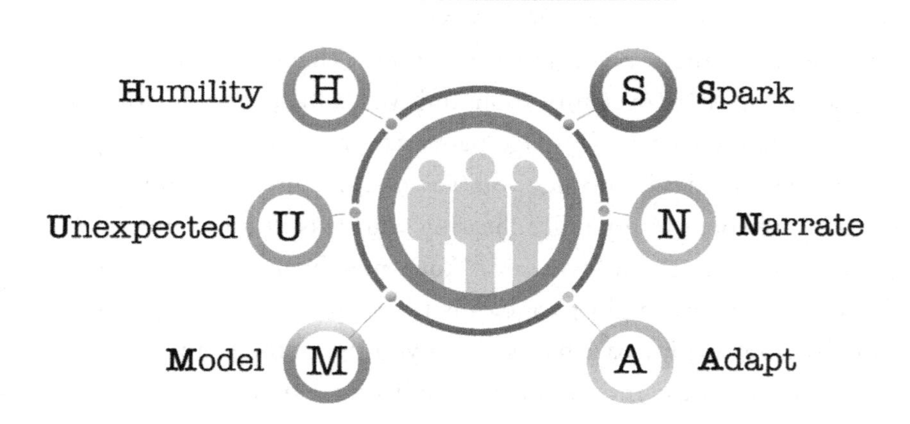

To download a more detailed "placemat" of the HUMANS framework, check out the "More Inspiration Hot Potatoes" section at the end of the book

• • • • • • •

People *respect*
authority
but they *follow*
authenticity.

• • • • • • • •

24

Uh, Cliff's Notes please

"To summarize the summary of the summary: people are a problem."

~ Douglas Adams - author, screenwriter, and someone who epitomized English humor

Okay, I know that was a hundred-mile-an-hour freight train of craziness. Welcome to my brain. So, let's slow down here for a second and do a quick recap of our journey thus far.

We started our voyage in Part 1 by affirming that something isn't quite right in your career. Your frustration with your existing work environment is justified. BS Burnout is real. And there is a way to successfully get through it. Your desire to have a seat at the table without compromising everything else is attainable. But we also agree (right?!) that taking the same ole approach you've taken up till now isn't going to get you there.

I introduced the concept of authenticity, the basis of how we'll turn everything around. However, authenticity isn't the passive, freewheeling idea you've subscribed to in the past. Authenticity is a much more nuanced and powerful concept. It's Greek origin, "authentikos," means to be genuine, original, and authoritative. It infers being authentic is an intersection between being yourself and being badass. I hope this fresh look at the word invoked your curiosity and helped you see it might be possible to use something as simple as authenticity as a foundation for your new career playbook.

From there, we did a little gentle sanding of your soul. In Part 2, we talked about the Sucky Songs you likely sing that are holding you back. I know it might have felt a little annoying, but we had to do this work first, otherwise nothing I taught you in Part 3 would stick around for long. While I highlighted the playlist I hear from most people (and have sung myself many times in my career), I encouraged you to recognize and rewrite other songs you might sing. This Sucky Song thing will be an ongoing process. These songs don't stop coming – I sang many of my own while writing this book – but what you're holding in your hands is a process to help you more quickly recognize them and rewrite them.

Then, in Part 3, we dove into the Six Principles of Strategic Authenticity, using the acronym HUMANS, and we looked at how each component can be applied to your work and to your life.

Humility

Unexpected

Model

Adapt

Narrate

Spark

First, we talked about **humility** and the concept of creating a Humility Halo. Humility allows you to connect more quickly, gain greater trust, and leave people intrigued and curious. I prompted you to list stories, traits, or other items in your life that you could use as moments of humility. Finally, I introduced a process called the Cycle of Humility that will help you continually identify, embrace, and share these humility moments.

Next, we talked about the power of being **unexpected**. I love this element the most. Being unexpected is a synonym for not doing things in the typical manner, which I believe is the only way we progress as individuals and as a society. We strive to be unexpected in business (it's called innovation!) but we don't innovate enough in how we act with others. I gave you an Unexpected Starter Kit — some ways you can start to surprise others by doing or saying something they don't expect. I also highlighted research that shows that when you do something unexpected, the other person's brain goes through a "surprise sequence," which makes them wake up, get curious, and prepare themselves to think differently. Being unexpected doesn't just gain you some attention, it's one of the best ways to ignite others to think more innovatively. I also talked about a few other "sur-prizes" being unexpected ushers in – creating humor and overcoming your underdog status. One of my favorite quotes comes from this section: "Watch what everyone else is doing. And then do the opposite."

Then we talked about the importance of **modeling**, that it's not just about what you say, it's about what you show. People seen as authentic often don't emit authenticity just through their words, they show it through their actions. We talked about the importance this has in the workplace and at home. In the end, it's all about making people *feel* what you expect them to do. Just like

I hope to do with this book. Yes, the words matter. But I hope the feeling matters more.

Next up, we talked about the concept of **adapting**. When I talk to people about authenticity, this pillar gives people the biggest "ah-ha." So often when people think about bringing more of their authenticity to work, they hit a brick wall (likely envisioning the first asshole they'll run into). But adapting to other people's authenticity is just as important. Does that mean if you're working with an asshole, you should be an asshole? Absolutely not. Instead, think about understanding how to best plug into each person you interact with and then let the other components of authenticity come out. For example, imagine making fun of a humble moment of yours when talking to a stuffy, egotistical colleague. It may seem risky, but chances are, it's the best strategy to inspire them to let loose a bit too.

We also talked about the importance of adapting your own authenticity. I introduced you to the concept of a Future Diary to help you focus more on defining who you *want* to be vs. who you *are*. I also shared one of my favorite and most powerful rules: The 50% Rule. This rule is great to lean on to ensure you're constantly growing. That is, be sure to take on each new assignment, role, or job only if it'll make you 50% uncomfortable. I encourage you to bookmark, write down, chant The 50% Rule! It's one of the simplest and most powerful guiding principles I can give to you.

Next, we talked about **narrating** (storytelling). This is another one of my favorites. Storytelling is one of the most powerful authenticity weapons you have. We talked about the power of storytelling and how stories are remembered twenty-two times more than facts. I busted down many of the barricades you likely have that hold you back from telling more stories at work. For example, it's only for the big stage, it takes up too much time. To get through these barriers, we talked about the many places you can start inserting stories at work. I suggested you create your own Story Inventory so that you have stories at the ready. Finally, I introduced the STORY Inventory (**S**imile, **T**weets, **O**ther people's stories, **R**elate, **Y**ours), which outlines the five different kinds of stories you can use at work.

And finally, we talked about **sparking** others, and how inspiration is like a game of Hot Potato. That is, as soon as you're inspired by someone or something, you have to throw it to someone else. And it's your job to always be playing the game. If you're not inspired, go seek out that inspiration. And if you're feeling it, be damn sure you give it back out to others ASAP! It might take decades for others to recognize the impact you've made. Sparking others to be and do more, including being more authentic, is not just my job, your leader's job, your parents' job. It's all our jobs. And it's the most important job you have.

PART 4

Who Says This Is The Top?

25 Proudest coaching moment ever

"Don't be afraid to give up the good to go for the great."

~ John D. Rockefeller - business magnate, philanthropist, and someone who figured out how to make a buck or two

I have an Uncle Bob. I imagine you might have your own version of an "Uncle Bob." Mine is a mashup of two Seinfeld icons. He acts like Kramer but is short like George Costanza. Growing up though, that never held him back. In high school he was a three-sport athlete and was even an all-state catcher. What he lacked in size, he overcame with speed. When his son, Matthew, was born, Uncle Bob couldn't wait to become Matthew's coach.

Although Matthew played just about every sport invented, if you ask Uncle Bob what his proudest coaching moment was, he'll tell you some version of this story:

> It was the annual Easter Egg Hunt at the Library House in Elk Rapids. Matthew was two years old and it was his first hunt. I was determined to coach him to be the best damn Easter egg hunter the town had ever seen. Everyone was lined

> up – parents and children, Easter baskets in hand. The energy in the air was electric. There was a shit ton of candy to be had, and every parent wanted their kid to "win." Now, Matthew was a bit undersized, so I knew it was my first test as his coach.
>
> I leaned down to Matthew and said, "See all of those Easter eggs right there?" (pointing to the sea of colorful eggs just twenty feet ahead of us). Matthew nodded with excitement. "Now Matthew, see that tree WAY off in the distance?" Matthew nodded again. "When they say 'go' I want you to run as fast as you can. And I don't want you to stop until you get to that tree. When you get to that tree, I want you to grab as many Easter eggs as you can."
>
> Three-Two-One-GO! The kids all took off running, their parents yelling and cheering them on. And do you know what happened when they all got to that first line of eggs? Every little body dropped as they scrambled to pick up a couple of eggs before the kids next to them got the rest. Every kid did this. Except Matthew.
>
> Matthew listened to me. While all the kids' heads were down, Matthew was running and running and running … and running. He ran until he got to that big oak tree way off in the distance, just like I had told him. As soon as he got there, he dropped to the ground and scooped and scooped and scooped up Easter eggs. That little kid had more Easter eggs than he could fit in his basket. I haven't had a prouder coaching moment since that day.

This story always makes me laugh. And it sticks with me on a much deeper level. *I* am Uncle Bob. *You* are Matthew. It's time for you to go on your own Easter Egg Hunt. All those other kids, competing for that first line of Easter eggs, that's what you've been doing at work. You've been working so damn hard, fighting for those Easter eggs among a sea of others. You keep running to the same line. You're using the same strategies for success as everyone else, which largely involves running and dropping hard and fast for the eggs that are in front of you. If you take only one key strategy away with you from our time together, I hope it's this: It's time to start doing things your own way.

Authenticity can be your path to a shit ton of Easter eggs.

I hope you now see that there isn't one path to get there. But there is one powerful strategy. When you're heading into your next Easter Egg Hunt, I want you to smile, take a deep breath, assess the situation, and use one thing you learned in this book. Then another. Then another.

And much like training wheels on a bike, at some point I want you to forget about the details of this book. I want you to stop referring to the HUMANS framework. I want you to release the training wheels. It will happen. My goal wasn't to change you. My goal was to get you excited and addicted to something new. Once you start seeing even small wins as you use authenticity as a strategy, you won't need much more than the feeling you're left with after reading this book. You'll only need the spark you were given – the guiding light that shone bright in the distance, highlighting that, by using your authenticity, you are guaranteed success.

26

I'm not a unicorn. You don't have to be one either.

"It is never too late to be what you might have been."

~ George Eliot - who was actually Mary Ann Evans,
a writer and authentic work in progress

I know that much of this book features my success and my conviction that authenticity worked for me. And I know you may have thought once or twice, *Yeah, this chick seems like she's pretty bold and outgoing; of course authenticity worked for her. But I'm not sure I can pull it off.*

Please throw that Sucky Song right out the window. I want to be sure you know that authenticity success stories are happening every day and they're coming from introverts and extroverts. They're coming from corporate types, entrepreneurs, and teachers. Stories are coming from big-ass executives and from individual contributors. They're happening everywhere to the people that have had the guts to simply take at least one new authentic step forward in their career.

I want to tell you just a few of the hundreds of stories that people have sent me since I started cheering on the authenticity movement a few years ago.

RENÉE BAUER, DIVORCE ATTORNEY AND CEO OF THE BAUER LAW GROUP

Renée has been a divorce attorney for many years, and she described her work life up to this point this way: "I've been doing my job, playing the part, and never sharing anything personal about my own divorce journey." She didn't want clients and other lawyers to know about her personal life because she didn't believe it was professional. She said, "You just don't do that. You stay buttoned up and on task."

Then one day, she felt like everything changed. She was interviewed on our *b Cause podcast,* and my co-host, Nicole, started asking Renée personal questions about her own divorce experience. Much to Renée's surprise, she answered. After the episode aired, she received countless messages from women thanking her for sharing her story because they were sitting in their own shame and guilt from their divorces. After that, Renée started talking about divorce in a different way. "I talked about shame and grief and guilt. I told people I was divorced not once but twice. People didn't stop hiring me, but rather, something crazy happened – my law firm got busier than ever, and my social media platform exploded."

This ultimately gave Renée the idea and courage to start another business, one that more broadly helps women with divorce education and coaching. She attributes this all to her seeing the power of authenticity. She says, "All of this came about because I started being authentic and letting people in rather than abiding by some rule that I thought I was supposed to follow in order to be taken seriously. I learned authenticity is the best way to do business."

HEATHER PIERCE, CORPORATE LEADER

Heather recently took on a new role within a Fortune 10 company, where she often leads large strategy sessions. She says, "The people that attend are primarily in senior level roles, including the COO and CEO of our local health plan. Needless to say, the meetings can be a bit intimidating. But this latest strategy session, I decided to add in a healthy dose of authenticity in a very thoughtful and strategic way."

First, she decided to demonstrate one of their business' core values – Keep Things Fun – by kicking off the meeting with a story about kayaking the Colorado River. "I told everyone about my adventure and talked about how important trips like that were for my physical and mental health. We're in the health care business after all, and wellness is a big part of our strategy."

Later in the meeting, when discussing details of a project with a health system in her local area, instead of talking facts and figures, Heather told a very personal story about her experience delivering her second son at the hospital. "I recalled a story about the student anesthesiologist I allowed to watch over my c-section. I talked about his incredible bedside manner, and I told the group that I would never forget him helping me get through it. I described the feeling I had when he said, 'Nice job, Mom' and high-fived me as they were sewing up my abdomen." Heather suggested that their goal as a team should be to create similar experiences for others.

After the meeting, several people came to Heather and told her how much they appreciated her approach and how it changed the tone of the meeting for the better. Heather says, "We have to remind each other we're humans and real people outside of these jobs. And outside of these jobs, our own decisions quite literally impact our personal lives."

KENDRA MONTSTREAM, LIBRARY MEDIA SPECIALIST/TEACHER

Kendra has been an educator for nineteen years in many roles, including classroom teacher, reading teacher, and special education teacher, and now she is a library media specialist. Though she felt like she was personally creative in every role, ultimately, she followed the rules and did what she was asked. She felt like her job was simply her job. Unlike in the business world, she felt like there was little room for being a leader, standing out, and creating change.

Kendra says, "I know I'm a great teacher, but I struggled with what I could do to have others see me as more than just that. I wondered, *How can I become a real asset and power for those around me?*" She went on to say, "Listening to Erin talk about how to take control of your own job, life, and vision, without sacrificing other things in life, must have sunk in a bit."

Kendra started to take a new approach at the beginning of the 2019–20 school year. She wanted her voice to be heard. She wanted more responsibility and to make a more significant impact on the school and the students. Kendra started suggesting ideas to her principal and vice principal. She networked. And she advocated for herself and the other teachers in the building. She became the go-to person for other teachers to voice their ideas, as they saw that she could help them make things happen.

She felt like she was on a roll … then March 13, 2020 happened. Like a lot of places in the world, the COVID-19 pandemic sent her school's teachers and students home. Kendra was now separated from the place that held the spark for so much of her creativity and forward momentum. Kendra's job also changed dramatically. "I now had to be a behind-the-scenes technology teacher. But I listened when Erin talked about how change can be scary but also rewarding. I felt down but not out. I decided to make my new job the best job."

Teachers continued to seek her out and others as well. Kendra became the go-to person for teachers, administrators, parents, and students … now through computer screens, text messages, and phone calls at all hours of the day and night, including weekends. "As I neared the end of the school year, I felt proud of myself. I knew I had essentially changed my job description in a matter of hours. I helped so many people and facilitated distance-learning work within my school."

But doubt still crept in. Who would notice all she was doing when everyone was quarantined in their own homes? In one of Kendra's final (virtual) meetings of the school year, they announced Teacher of the Year. "I was ready to congratulate the teacher who would get this honor in this unprecedented year. And, well, it was me! In my twentieth year of teaching, in the crazy year that was 2020, I received the award!"

As they read off the reasons she was selected, people mentioned all the things she thought no one would notice she had done. "You couldn't have given me enough money in the world to replace having my colleagues tell me how invaluable I had been to them and the school. And it was all because I finally understood and received the permission to be more of who I am, even when people didn't ask me to. This is now the greatest power I have."

MEGAN THATFORD, CEO OF ELITE MEET

After years in marketing and advertising, both at large corporations and then later running her own marketing and communications company, Megan found her calling: to support military-based organizations. Although Megan has never been in the military herself, she has been surrounded by veterans all her life. Her father, brother, and many others around her helped her appreciate the sacrifice, impact, and challenges that our active and retired military personnel face.

Megan was supporting several military-focused nonprofits through her marketing company, Minot Marketing Communications. One day she received a call she couldn't have anticipated. Elite Meet, a nonprofit organization for Special Operations veterans, which transitions people from the military into civilian careers, asked her to become their next CEO. Megan recalls getting this offer, saying, "This is an organization with over one thousand elite veterans, members of the Special Operations Forces (SOF) and fighter pilot community. These are people that have seen more, accomplished more, and endured more than I can ever imagine. Naturally, the opportunity to lead and support this community was a huge honor. Then it hit me ... the insecurity, the fear, the very real effects of imposter syndrome. I knew I was qualified to lead the organization, but I had significant concerns about how I going to be received by the members."

Megan took the role. But she knew she'd need to take a different approach. "The camaraderie within the SOF community is unique. I knew it was unlikely that I would be accepted into the organization in the same way a veteran would be because I've never served in the military. I knew I needed to gain the confidence of the members in my own way. I knew that meant being authentic."

Megan's first large-scale interaction with the organization's members was a virtual town hall that she led. "I was honestly quite nervous. I don't really like being in the limelight. I decided though that instead of trying to 'fake it,' I would instead use authenticity as my strategy. I started off by telling the group, 'This is NOT a stuffy corporate town hall.' I told them that the intention of the event was to hear their feedback and get to know them. And if I was in fact going to truly get to know them, I needed to see them. So, I decided to call out each one of them by name, with a lighthearted tone, and then requested they put their camera on."

Her strategy worked. The light banter about things like being camera-shy lightened the mood and prompted casual conversation. After her business update, the members shared their stories and ideas. She put herself on mute to listen (and drown out her barking dog too, of course). When she decided to chime in again, she was still on mute. "Members let me know I was on mute. But instead of freaking out, I joked and said, 'What would a virtual event be without someone trying to talk when they are on mute?' I could see the smiles and giggles. I could see the smiles because everyone was ON camera. As I observed their reactions, I knew that my authenticity had won them over."

Megan's passion for supporting the veteran community is what drives her every day. She's realized that it isn't just her passion and strong work ethic that is fueling her success. She now eagerly accepts the challenge of being a non-military leader of a military-focused organization. In fact, the more intimidating, the more exciting it's become for her. "It turns out, I'm very much like the veterans I serve. These qualities of determination, hard work, and commitment are embodied in the members of the SOF community. All I needed to do for them to accept me was lead as me, li'l ole four-foot-ten civilian, patriotic, devoted me. As the members see my passion and drive, I've become respected. I want the members to see me not as some stuffy CEO, but as Megan, another human that genuinely cares about their success, and someone that will lead the organization with their best interests in mind."

SARAH HAVERKAMP, CORPORATE LEADER

Sarah was asked to take part in a training video series for the sales team at her company. Sarah says (sarcastically), "I was the lucky one who got assigned to record a module on member engagement. I dreaded the exercise. While presenting to clients is natural to me, recording myself is a whole different beast."

Sarah sat down to record her video. She recorded. She deleted. She recorded again. She deleted again. "I think I recorded myself fifty times," Sarah said. "I was so self-conscious, thinking to myself, this is SO boring that I don't even want to hear this."

She continued to record over and over for the next few hours. Then, she had an epiphany. Sarah decided that instead of trying to make a "perfect" video, she would simply record what she was thinking about as she was going through the video-making process. She told me, "I was my authentic self. I told the audience that this was awkward for me and likely boring for them because my video was one of their last modules to get through, but we were going to get through this together. I was channeling what I think you would coach me to do."

She completed and submitted her video, but over the weekend, she started to feel self-conscious about what she'd done. Yet several days later, she got a note from someone on the sales team telling her they thought her module was the best one – the most engaging and entertaining. Sarah said, "Thank you – without your guidance, I don't think I would have been brave enough to speak what I was feeling inside (which I hope they never ask me to do again … LOL!)."

27 There's no time like the present

"The pandemic has heightened our fears and lowered our standards."

~ Me

There is no better time than right now to adopt authenticity as your new career strategy. I'm writing this part of the book smack-dab in the middle of the COVID-19 pandemic in 2020. I've found writing really comforting during lockdown. But don't worry, I'm not THAT annoying, perfectionist who has it all together. Perhaps like mine, your life is a bit of a shit-show. My children are homeschooling (they're twelve and nine years old). My business is being slapped around a bit. My house is a jail cell. And at the same time, I've been incredibly driven to write this book. Catch this: For my Mother's Day present, I asked for two quiet hours alone to write.

I feel like the pandemic is the tailwind for bringing more authenticity to the workplace. Authenticity barriers have been coming down like the Berlin Wall. The amount of authentic messiness that the quarantine has ushered into our lives is un-be-liev-able. Zoom calls with executives (and famous people) with their kids running in and out. Commercials filmed from employees' couches. Because we've been dealt something so incredibly unusual, the entire world has been forced to be more authentic. It's like we've all been bottling up this desire to stop putting on facades and pretending that we can perfectly juggle our crazy work and personal lives. It took an impossible situation to finally allow us all to exhale what we've been holding in for so many years, maybe even a lifetime: We are human. We have messy thoughts and imperfect lives, that, until this time, we largely haven't exposed at work. And it's our job – yours and mine (and I hope millions of others) – to make sure it continues.

I am sincerely excited for you. I hope you feel the same butterflies I do. I hope this book has helped you get excited about a new way forward. I hope you see the light at the end of the tunnel. Actually, no. I hope you light that frickin' tunnel on fire! I hope you've seen that there is a way to punch that asshole that keeps pushing the Up button on your work treadmill. I hope you see that you can go to work and be bold and brave and different. I hope you see there is a way to fundamentally change the workplace for you ... and for others.

28

We need a whole bunch of A-HOLEs

"Don't be afraid of being different.
Be afraid of being the same as everyone else."

~ Unknown

Twenty plus years ago, I failed miserably attempting to become an actuary. Was I not quite smart enough for those insane math exams? Maybe. But more than that, I absolutely hated sitting in a room for hours, studying by myself. It was an individual sport. Writing a book is also an individual sport. In fact, I can't believe I made it to this point! While I've been supported by an incredible book coach, I have been largely doing this ALL. BY. MYSELF.

I am a team-sport kinda girl. I played and coach basketball. Yes, I love the high of swishing a three-point shot through the hoop. But way more than that, I love the concept of being part of a team. I love the adrenaline rush of the pre-game shenanigans. I love celebrating a win together. That's what I want here.

Let me be straight: I didn't leave my fancy, high-flying, pretty darned lucrative corporate job to become an entrepreneur and help a few people. I left so I could affect millions. And the only way I can do that is by creating an inspiration platform. (Recall: This is a key component of the Spark in HUMANS, and I practice what I preach.)

So how do we do that? Well, as I mentioned earlier, part of that is me asking you to pay it forward. Asking you to tell your stories, be a beacon for others, spread the authenticity love. But remember, I also don't preach *normal.* Telling stories and being a beacon sounds kinda normal. We need to do more. And we need to have fun while doing it.

That's why I started A-HOLEs. I wanted a name to unite us. An energy to drive us. Something ridiculous to make us laugh. And, well, an inside joke that helps keep us all from losing our minds!

A-HOLE stands for **A**uthentic **H**umans **O**verhauling **L**ousy **E**nergy. At the end of the day, that's what we're all setting out to do. We are collectively heading out on a voyage to covertly re-program the working world at large. The workplace is loaded with lousy energy. Just sit on those two words for a minute – lousy energy. I'm sure you can think of at least three people, recent meetings, or situations that *totally* meet that definition. Maybe it was your manager who told you to take something "offline." Or was it the dude that pushed you to create 213 versions of a PowerPoint deck (with the perfect font and new-age icon bullets) only to unveil in the meeting that he wasn't going to do a page-turn? Is it the person that couldn't be bothered turning on their camera for a Zoom call, even though you ran around like a mad-person this morning to make sure you showered and put on a shirt and pants?

This lousy energy is all a product of this decades-old, fake(ish) working world vortex that we've been caught in. And the best way to get out of that vortex is to create a whole new energy to overtake it and rewire the frequency in which we all work and live.

So where do you start? How do you jump onto team A-HOLE?

By taking a Mad-Lib(ish) quiz to create your own customized A-HOLE Manifesto! This manifesto is like a flint to your fire, reminding you that you are special. You can create this manifesto by answering a few fun questions at https://www.bauthenticinc.com/a-hole-manifesto.

I'd love to have you become an A-HOLE!

29 Be your own prince(ss)

"It's weird to not be weird."

~ John Lennon - egg man, walrus, and Beatle

Back in the 1980s, the Rolling Stones were full-fledged kings of the music world. They'd been strutting their authentic music around since the '60s, propelling a whole new counterculture forward, and to this day, are one of music's most iconic and best-selling bands. In 1981, Mick Jagger noticed a new, unconventional singer in the business and asked him to open up for them at their Los Angeles shows.

It was a disaster.

The stadium was filled with nearly a hundred thousand fans when this new artist took the stage. He was wearing a see-through trench coat, tall black boots, and a black bikini. As he started to crank on his guitar and bust out his unusual falsetto voice, the crowd started booing him. Then they did more than boo him, and mayhem broke out. Food fights began and homophobic comments were chanted. One of the Rolling Stones recalled getting hit with a bag of fried chicken and then his guitar was struck by a grapefruit. And after four songs, the manager decided to pull the strange new artist from the stage.

That opening singer? Prince.

I'm pretty sure I don't have to tell you the rest of that story. What's most important is that Prince didn't change a thing about his act – his clothing style, his music, his authenticity – even after he had thousands of people strongly indicating he should. This will happen to you. Or at times, you'll predict it *might* happen to you. Surely it won't be people throwing food at you. But it could be other things. It could be strange looks from a mentor you admire. Or it could be an interview that goes a bit sideways.

Keep being authentic, even when people look at you like you're a weirdo.

Fight through it. You are leading, not following. And people will follow.

You were put on this earth for a reason. I'm certain you also want to make an impact. You're here to live up to your highest, truest self. You're here to shake things up and move things forward.

And make no mistake, that sounds glorious but often feels nebulous. Using authenticity – in its most nuanced and richest way – can help you crystallize that hazy feeling, hold it in your hand and take steps towards the career and life you've always wanted. Authenticity will support you transcending learning modules and buzzwords and bullshit, and instead, make simple changes every day that motivate people to be talking about you. Promoting you. Following you. Emulating you. Loving you.

And yes, there will be a few haters (mostly people who are jealous of your badassery), but even haters need help. Many of those who start as haters might even turn into disciples.

Using authenticity as your new playbook — your new secret weapon — will change everything. I promise. Watch as you start to think things like *Wow, I didn't even work that hard and got incredible results.* Or *Hmm, that leader never even knew my name, and now she's recommending me for major projects.* This will happen. And it will happen quickly. People are so freakin' ready for the freshness you're going to bring to work. They need it desperately. And most don't even know that's what they need. Be a beacon of hope not just for your career but for the millions of people who are burnt out, fed up, and let down by their colleagues, their careers, and their companies.

Get fired up, my friend. This is the turning point you've been waiting for. Bask in all its shiny glory and fun. Revel in the new energy you'll have. Soak in the money and success. Be authentic. Do it your own way.

Who says this is the top?

I conquered some big mountains. The struggling company I joined had a complete turnaround. Employees who were once deflated and frustrated were beaming with pride and joy. This was a company that used to barely tread water financially and was unable to invest in itself and grow. Yet we tripled our earnings in just three years and invested significantly in the growth of the business.

I learned and failed and triumphed and evolved my own authentic self over those last several years in corporate. Just when things were going incredibly well, an angel, as well as a devil, showed up on my shoulders.

Angel: You did it, kid! You deserve this easier time. The fire drills have largely gone away. Your team is so happy and loves you dearly. Your professional reputation is soaring because of it all. Enjoy. This. Time.

Devil: You're getting lazy, kid. You're not the same firecracker you once were. You know what you need, don't you? You need a new challenge.

I'd been learning and evolving my authenticity over the previous several years. And while I was still learning, it wasn't at the pace that I craved. I yearned to be able to listen to the angel voice, but my devil voice always won. I knew from years of experience that I had to listen to the devil.

Around the same time this was all running in my head, I went on a business trip. At the airport, I struck up a conversation in the Southwest Airlines cattle-call line with a very nice woman. We decided to continue our conversation and sit next to each other on the plane. She told me about how she had left the corporate world many years before to start her own company. She beamed with happiness and inspiration. I was intrigued.

After peppering her with a million questions, I paused and decided to admit why I was so inquisitive. I confessed that I was contemplating my next career move. I told her that, much to my surprise, I was thinking it might not be at the company I had spent my career at thus far. I shared with her that I thought I must be crazy to consider doing something like that, especially at this time. My reputation was at an all-time high. I was sitting on a peak I never imagined I'd be able to reach.

After rambling on for a bit. I stopped to take in her reaction. That's when she looked at me and so quickly, succinctly, and matter-of-factly said, "Who says this is the top?"

Who says this is the top?

That one sentence left one of the most impactful marks in my soul. I envisioned a mountain range. In seconds I became fearful of never knowing what the view looked like from atop another peak. I couldn't imagine going through life without exploring the terrain – the pricker bushes and the flowers – that lined the path up those other mountains. Massive fear was overwhelming me.

What if I never saw what was on the other side of this mountain?

What if there was something even more beautiful to climb?

What if I had only just begun to develop into the authentic person I was meant to be?

Nine months later I announced my retirement. I decided to hike up another mountain. I decided to make spreading the power of authenticity my next mountain climb. And I hope you will too.

Never stop climbing.

The Real(ish) Preface

I remember the day I told my business coach I wanted to start writing this book. She cringed and said, "Erin, you've got so much going on right now. It might be too much."

Clearly, I didn't buy into my coach's attempt at caution.

My desire to write this book wasn't coming from my typical Type-A, get-er-done drive. This book felt like a gremlin trying to claw its way out of me. After so many years seeing thousands of people feeling burnt out, fed up, and let down in their careers, I knew I had to share my story and more importantly my formula for success. A formula that helped me have success without selling out.

I also had no shortage of ironic moments during my writing journey. The first came as I was determining the name of the book. As most authors do, I obsessed over finding the perfect name. In one coaching group I'm part of, they even taught us a formula for titling books. After running my concept through their formula, this book *should* have been called *Success without Selling Out*. Except, that didn't feel … authentic. In fact, our b Cause Facebook group (a supercharged group of authenticity junkies) called me out hard on this, several people leaving me comments like "You preach authenticity, and that book name is so not authentic to you, Erin!" In fact, *You Do You(ish)* wasn't even a title my book coach really liked, but in the end, I knew there was nothing more important than a book name that embodied the principles I outline within its pages. So, I went against the norm, just like I teach in this book, and named it my own way.

There were many instances like this while I was writing *You Do You(ish)*. Even though I preach and teach doing things your own way, I got myself regularly wrapped up in believing I had to follow the "classic" book-writing playbook. I got lost in how other authors did things. I got discouraged because they wrote more poetically or used bigger words. I also got twisted around an axle on things like word count, cover design, and how I would launch and market my book. I sent myself on a rollercoaster of highs (Yes, I'm doing it my own way!) and lows (I suck at this!). Every time I stepped off the rollercoaster, I would look up, laugh at the irony, and reset my resolve to write this book *authentically*.

I also had one of my bucket-list items happen while I was in the middle of writing this book. I was selected to do a TEDx Talk in October 2020. So, despite my natural tendency to keep pushing through, I decided to push writing aside for several months to focus on my TEDx Talk. (Truth be told, my book coach strong-armed me to put it aside, giving me the critical guidance that I could not do both at the same time and do either well. I'm forever grateful to her for that.)

The TEDx Talk "interruption" ended up being a true blessing. Not only did it slow me down and force me to write a richer book but I also learned a critical lesson: The real power isn't in what you say, it's in what you *don't* say. Writing the foundation of my talk was easy. It was the shaping, molding, and cutting of things (that I so wanted to say) that was the most difficult part. But it was that very process that helped me deliver a talk that truly told the story people needed to hear. Then I brought that lesson back to my writing here. This book is about 30% shorter than what I started with. While I certainly don't suffer a word shortage, I realized the most important thing I could do was to take the time to ensure I gave you just the right amount of inspiration and guidance you need to make a massive shift. Nothing more. Nothing less.

Finally, I have to acknowledge the intensity of the time surrounding us all while I wrote this book – the COVID-19 pandemic. While there is much I could say here, the truth is that writing this book was a solace for me. Without a pandemic, this book would not exist. It was the long drawn-out nature of the pandemic that most left me *needing* to write this book ... for myself as well as for all of you. I have limited patience for doing things that take a long time. Writing a book is a time-consuming thing. No way around it. And the pandemic is unfortunately also a time-consuming thing. No way around it. This odd marriage of time-consuming things was the mental woobie blanket I needed to help me through this tough time. I hope you, too, can find your own mental blanket during these difficult times. And if this book is a tiny piece of it, I will be so frickin' happy.

Discussion Guide

- What were your impressions on the author's style? Did you find the book easy to read or a slog?
- Of all the information presented in *You Do You(ish)*, what stayed with you the most?
- Why do you think the workplace is so inauthentic today? What do you think we need to do to change it more systematically?
- Did you agree with the author's definition of authenticity? Where do you deviate?
- Which Sucky Song did you relate to the most?
- Did you identify a Sucky Song for yourself that wasn't in the book?
- Have you been able to rewrite any Sucky Songs since reading the book?
- Do you think you can be authentic at work? Does your answer change based on the author's definition of the word?
- Which letter of the HUMANS (Humility, Unexpected, Model, Adapt, Narrate, Spark) framework changed your mindset the most?
- Did reading the book affect your optimism for your career? If yes, how so?
- What one thing taught in this book are you most skeptical about?

- What one immediate change did you make as a result of reading *You Do You(ish)*?
- Who is your Authentic North Star?
- What aspect of the author's story could you most relate to?
- If you could ask the author one thing, what would it be?
- How does the book's title work in relation to its contents? If you could give the book a new title, what would it be?
- Did *You Do You(ish)* remind you of any other books?
- How did it affect you? Do you think you'll remember it in a few months or years?
- Share a favorite quote from the book. Why did this quote stand out?
- Who do you most want to read this book?

Resources in the Book

1. Justin Wolfers, *Fewer Women Run Big Companies Than Men Named John* (nytimes.com: 2015)
2. Jim Harter, *U.S. Employee Engagement Reverts Back to Pre-COVID-19 Levels* (gallup.com: 2020)
3. Paul Zak, *The Neuroscience of Trust* (hbr.org: 2017)
4. Frances X. Frei and Anne Morriss, *Begin with Trust* (hbr.org: 2020)
5. Jim Harter and Annmarie Mann, *The Right Culture: Not Just About Employee Satisfaction* (gallup.com: 2017)

More Inspiration Hot Potatoes

Here are some free resources to give you even more weapons for career success:

- To see me "stir the pot" on the TEDx Farmingdale stage, watch my TEDx Talk titled, "Why you don't have to compromise for your career"
- Are you a podcast junkie (virgins are always welcome too!) who would dig some real-time career advice plus a healthy dose of authentic humor? Check out our *b Cause podcast* @ https://www.bauthenticinc.com/podcast
- Feeling stuck in your current job and want a step-by-step guide on how to get unstuck? Check out my mini-course, "Unst*ck Yourself" at https://bauthenticinc.mykajabi.com/unstuck-yourself-home
- For articles that will help you tackle everything from rocking your performance review to finding your purpose in life, check out my blog at https://www.bauthenticinc.com/our-2-cents
- To download a one-page "placemat" of the HUMANS framework to help you keep *doing* authentic on a regular basis, go to: https://bauthenticinc.mykajabi.com/humans
- For companies looking for a speaker, my 90-min Authenticity Awakening, or some totally authentic training, please contact me @ hello@bauthenticinc.com.

About Me (Yes, I Wrote This Too)

I'm a career coach, TEDx and keynote speaker, podcast co-host, author, MBA, runner, wife, mom of two, and someone who just really loves to dance where I'm not supposed to.

In Fall 2018, I decided to leave what was arguably a dream job. After leading a storybook turnaround of a company with about one thousand people and $2 billion in assets, I decided to walk away from it all.

Why? I was yearning for a new mountain to climb. But shortly after I left, I realized I was put on this earth for a unique reason: to eradicate the working world of all its BS. (Well, maybe not all, but to take a healthy chunk out of it.) I founded b Authentic inc (bauthenticinc.com) and have since become a nationally sought-after expert in authenticity in the workplace. My 2020 TEDx Talk dropped a truth bomb on conventional thinking about gender inequality, purporting that we're trying to solve it the wrong way. No surprise, I argue that authenticity is the solution to gender inequality in corporate spaces, plus so much more.

I love to speak to audiences and make them laugh, think, and take immediate IGW action. I've spoken in front of audiences as big as six hundred to as small as two (my kids – ha ha!). I also love to coach people, focusing primarily on high-potential, overachieving women who are hitting a wall that's preventing them from getting the career they deserve. I'm also a regular contributor to Business Week and have been featured on television and various publications, always finding a way to spread the power of authenticity. But my most audacious venture is hosting an edu-taining podcast that is focused on career, comedy, and community. It's called *b Cause with Erin & Nicole.* Come for me, stay for Nicole.

The granddaddy of accomplishments in my life all started out with a teeny bit of workplace flirting back in 1999. I was in the midst of failing at my final actuarial exam. At the same time, I was succeeding at my first (and only) husband exam. I met Manny in one of my earliest jobs, and after months of flirting and a kiss in a hot tub with my bathing suit on inside out, he became my boyfriend. Four years later we were married. Several years after that we created two of the coolest humans on the face of this earth, Ella and Mick. And yes, they are growing up as authentic as authentic can be.

LinkedIn: @Erin-Hatzikostas
Instagram: @erinhatzikostas
Facebook: @b Authentic inc
Twitter: @ErinHatzikostas, @bcausepodcast

Acknowledgments

It's ironic that I'm sitting down to write my thank-yous on a rainy Saturday afternoon, snuggled up on the couch with my favorite blanket, laptop, and a college football game on the TV. Meanwhile, my husband has spent the last three hours out in the 45-degree rain, getting our house ready for the winter.

To Manny — my husband, best friend, and the father of our beautifully authentic children — thank you for giving me the space and grace I needed to write this book. More importantly, thank you for never once questioning my decision to leave my stable and lucrative career to climb a new mountain. I am beyond grateful.

To my father, for giving me the DNA and the "business case" for the power of authenticity. You were my number-one model – your stories, sense of humor, and insatiable desire to do things your own way are the reasons for my success.

To my mother, for being the best mom on the planet. You have always — even now when I am forty-six years old — ensured I feel safe, loved, and supported. You are the yin to Dad's and my yang. I love you.

To the leaders that most shaped my career: Lisa Cararra, for giving me my first "figure shit out" job and being a beautifully authentic human. Martha Temple, for taking a chance on me and handing me my first "big girl" job. You were my first proof that corporate executives can be authentic and have success. Dan Finke, for a phone call of support I'll never forget (after a not-so-authentic call) and for being the most approachable, laid-back senior leader I know.

To Karen Lynch for being the most powerful sponsor in my corporate career. You might not know it, but the permission you gave me to be *me* during our first meeting in Omaha changed everything. I am in awe (as are so many others) as you continue to take a jackhammer to the corporate glass ceiling.

And to my other big career sponsor, Renee Zaugg. You are a complete badass, and I'll forever be grateful for the great work we got to do together (and I'm also secretly hoping, now that you're the CIO of Otis, you'll figure out how to add an Undo button to elevators. So needed!)

To Jean LaTorre for your intellect, style, and authenticity and for providing the flashlight I needed to see just how to be an executive and a cool chick at the same time.

They say that you are the average of the people you spend the most time with. These humans are the reason I was able to maintain the vibrational frequency needed to write a book:

Nicole Licata Grant: my podcast co-host, friend, and one of the most hilarious humans on the planet. Thank you for your sincere and never-ending support. The fact that we haven't killed each other after two years recording a podcast is proof that we were meant to do big things together.

Megan Thatford: one of the most caring human beings I know. Who would have known that when we met just a few years ago that our friendship would run this deep, this quickly? Thank you for always cheering me on and being there for me.

Kaitlyn Czapiga: my former nanny turned friend and spiritual North Star. Although the pandemic has lessened our time together, your magical energy will live in me forever.

Rick Courchaine: you have been one of my biggest supporters since the minute I started my entrepreneurial ventures. Thank you for the countless hours of work you've done for me and your overall support. I owe you more than you know.

Rachel Salgado: thank you for coming into my business and life. Without your incredible ability to master everything I throw your way and turn messes into magic, I wouldn't have been able to focus on what was most important: writing a great book.

Jess Sobieralski, Barret Katuna, Karen DeCorleto, Jenn Barnett: Our morning runs are my church. You are my pastors. Thank you for being the physical and mental spark I needed to write this book … and to do life in general.

Patti M Hall — Ironically, words can't even begin to describe how grateful I am for you. Formally my book coach, you are so much more than that. I cannot imagine going on this journey with anyone else. You taught me so much more than how to write a book. You dove deep into my soul to ensure I wrote a book to my highest, most authentic power.

To Dino Marino for putting up with Patti's and my craziness and pulling together the best-looking book possible. Your calm and steadfast nature is appreciated more than you know.

And to Paula Chiarcos, my amazing copy editor, for not just whipping my commas and parentheses into shape, but for caring for the book more than I expected and helping me make it the best it could be.

To the *You Do You(ish)* board: Jason Beach, Barbara Flitsch, Felicia Betancur, Melissa Patrone, Marissa Krupski, Nicole Licata Grant, Rafat Fields, and Rick Courchaine. Thank you for giving up so many evenings to help shape the launch of this book. You all are some of my favorite people, and I will be forever grateful for your support.

To all our peeps in the *b Cause podcast* Facebook group, thank you for your continuous feedback on everything from the book title to the cover to the contents. You never once gave me lip service. That is true authenticity.

Lastly, to my favorite two humans on the planet: Ella and Mick. Thank you for inspiring me every day. Keep doing things your own way. I love you more.

Made in the USA
Middletown, DE
18 February 2021